LeadAbility™

Transforming the Way
We Live and Work Together

Dr. Wade A. McNair

with Tony Rosback

Technics Publications

BASKING RIDGE, NEW JERSEY

Published by:

 TECHNICS PUBLICATIONS
TECHNOLOGY / LEADERSHIP

2 Lindsley Road
Basking Ridge, NJ 07920 USA
https://www.TechnicsPub.com

Cover design by Lorena Molinari
Graphics design by Sydney Sanchez
Edited by Sadie Hoberman

First Printing 2019
Copyright © 2019 by Wade A. McNair

ISBN, print ed.   9781634625999
ISBN, Kindle ed.   9781634626002
ISBN, ePub ed.   9781634626019
ISBN, PDF ed.   9781634626026

Library of Congress Control Number: 2019948079

Contents

CONTENTS

Acknowledgements

- To Jordan, my daughter, for her unwavering support and always challenging me to be better today than yesterday, and better tomorrow than today. Thank you.

- To Tony, my contributing author and the team at AmeriGas for their commitment to making work life better for those they lead. Thank you.

- To my Dad, the first leader in my life and one that demonstrated everyday what it means to positively influence others. Thank you.

- To Sydney Sanchez, our Instructional Designer for her expertise in designing the graphics, training, and tools for this edition. Thank you.

- To Ty Lusk, for his hard work and attention to detail in the drafting and editing of the manuscript. Thank you.

- To Dr. David Wilkinson at The Oxford Review for his commitment to academic excellence and providing ongoing research support for practitioners like myself. Thank you.

- Finally, to Steve Hoberman, our publisher, for his guidance and support in our efforts to publish the book now in your hands. Thank you.

About the Author

Wade A. McNair, Psy.D.

Dr. McNair is a dynamic Coach, Consultant, and Communicator with over 20 years of experience in Talent Management, Corporate Learning, HR, Leadership, and Organization Development.

Wade is actively engaged in coaching and consulting with corporate, non-profit, and faith-based organizations. In addition to his professional practice, Wade is an Adjunct Professor at both the undergraduate and graduate levels. Wade has a Master's Degree in Organizational Leadership and a Doctorate of Psychology in Organizational Management and Change.

Wade's personal mission is to "live and help others live authentic lives where our actions and behaviors are in alignment with our assumptions and beliefs." He resides in Orange County, CA with his daughter Jordan, and their miniature schnauzer, Rory.

Tony Rosback [Contributer]

Mr. Rosback has over 20 years' experience in leading diverse teams and organizations. Tony has been Vice President and Chief Operating Officer of AmeriGas Propane since March 2015.

Tony came to AmeriGas from Williams Scotsman, Inc., a mobile and modular space and storage solution company, where he served as Senior Director of West Region Operations and North American Logistics from 2014 to 2015. From 2013 to 2014, he was Senior Vice President and General Manager of the west for The Brickman Group Ltd., a commercial landscaping and property maintenance company.

From 2006 to 2013, Tony held various positions at Republic Services Inc. including Area President, Regional Vice President of Operations, Vice President of Operations Support and Market Vice President. From 1999 to 2006, Tony served as an Assistant Vice President at Cintas Corporation, a provider of uniforms, first aid, and safety and fire protection products and services.

About this Book

What makes a Leader?

What probably comes immediately to mind is a person that is bold, self-assured, and charismatic or has some other set of traits associated with high-profile and well-known leaders.

In 1954, Dr. Cattell set out "to determine the traits which characterize an effective leader." His research revealed a set of traits that were believed to be innate, supporting the notion that leaders are born, and therefore only some people are destined for leadership. This view of leadership as an inborn set of traits has existed for some time.

However, my 20 years' experience consulting and coaching leaders has made something very clear to me – EVERYONE has the potential to effectively lead others. Furthermore, research is supporting the wider view of leadership being an ability and a set of behavioral choices – well beyond the limitations of a "naturally born leader".

As such, I am passionate about reframing the conversation about leadership. Working with amazing organizations like AmeriGas, we developed a new leadership framework called "A Better Leader Model".

Instead of a focus on the nouns "leader" and "manager" we will focus our efforts on understanding what it takes "to lead" and "to manage" effectively based on real-world experience, sound science, and common sense.

As you read through this book, remember to ask yourself the following questions:

- Who am I being?
- How does this information impact me in the real world?
- How can I apply what I am reading to the personal and organizational leadership challenges I face?

Join us on this journey, where leadership is a choice and an ability that can be learned and developed by everyone.

All the best!

- W -

Understanding LeadAbility

Results and Relationships

Until recently, Management was considered the only "real" skillset needed in business and Leadership was a "nice to have". Management focused on getting Results whereas Leadership was focused on building Relationships. The tables have since turned and now Leadership is viewed as the essential skillset, prioritizing the building of Relationships, and Management's myopic focus on Results is relegated to the "old ways" of doing things.

As an Organizational Psychologist, I can tell you that BOTH are critical to creating and sustaining effective teams and organizations. In fact, both skill sets are essential to success in our personal lives as well. As such, we will present Leadership and Management from an Integrated Mindset rather than an "us vs. them" adversarial approach.

Our leadership definition integrates both management theory and leadership theory. Management theory usually focuses on the direction needed to achieve desired results, whereas Leadership theory usually focuses on the positive influence needed to achieve desired results.

By integrating the two – Results and Relationships – we create the expectations that to develop our LeadAbility we need both "Leaders as Managers" and "Managers as Leaders". Each of us needs to demonstrate the abilities of both building Relationships and getting Results – by influencing others and providing direction in our work and in our personal lives.

Leadership Defined

The word "Leadership" has multiple meanings and applications. There are probably as may definitions of what a leader is as there are leaders to give their opinion. In our efforts to integrate leadership and management, and establish a foundation for this book, we have chosen to define a Leader as someone that:

**Demonstrates the ability to positively influence behaviors
and provides the needed direction to achieve desired results.**

With this definition in mind, we further define "LeadAbility" as the ability to positively influence behaviors and provide the needed direction to achieve desired results.

Often organizations limit their levels of leadership to only those in supervisory or management roles. However, we believe every person in an organization has the ability to positively influence the behaviors of co-workers, teams, customers and partners. We also believe that every person has the ability to provide needed direction into their own work as well as the work of teams, customers, and partners. This mindset applies to our personal lives as well. With these definitions and mindsets, EVERYONE is a Leader and can grow and develop their LeadAbility.

Underlying Principles and Assumptions

Anytime we share a new model or training tool, it is important that we make sure we are starting on the same page with our underlying principles and assumptions.

First, LeadAbility is an Ability. It is a competency or capability that can be developed, grown, and mastered. By understanding how we experience leadership, we gain confidence and feel better equipped in our ability to influence and provide direction. By also understanding how others experience leadership, we are able to improve our relationships and help our teams and organizations more effectively reach desired results.

Second, LeadAbility is a Choice. LeadAbility is not only a skill we can develop, it is also a conscious choice we can make in response to the people and changes that occur in our lives and workplaces. The choice needs to start with our own awareness and a commitment to be a better leader. Every day we are faced with opportunities to influence others – the question is whether our influence will be positive. Every day we are faced with situations that require direction and the choice is ours as to what our impact will be. Ultimately, our ability to positively influence and provide needed direction, our LeadAbility, is a choice.

Third, LeadAbility is a Journey. There is no magic spell or miracle pill that can make a person suddenly lead more effectively. LeadAbility starts with a willingness to learn and a desire to grow in our own skills and abilities. If we do not take the time to understand our own experiences with leadership, it makes it difficult to show understanding, respect, and compassion for others. LeadAbility requires experiences for us to learn from, to journey through, and form the foundation we need to build our skill and competence.

As you read through this book, ask yourself these questions: Who am I being? Am I building the skill of LeadAbility? Am I choosing to purposefully be a positive influence or am I hindering or even hurting others in my choices? Am I effectively providing insight and direction, or am I allowing leadership opportunities to pass by? These questions start your journey. And as you move through this book, you are encouraged to not just understand the concepts, but to move beyond the information and apply it to your real life.

LeadAbility and Established Psychological Theory

Leadership has been an interest of study for centuries. Early Romans, Greeks, and other ancient cultures had their history and lore based on qualities of leadership and specific leadership roles within their civilization. An entire book could be written just on the history of leadership and management theory; however, we will cover just the major thought eras in the last two centuries. Each set of theories builds upon the previous, so the theories and related research has been an ongoing evolution rather than a specific shift in leadership philosophy.

Great Man Theory (1840)

The focus here is on leader as hero, that leaders are born and not made. Thomas Carlyle in 1840 created the term and the theory that leadership was limited to only a few that were born with the unique abilities to effectively lead others. Herbert Spencer later expressed a contrasting view that heroic leaders are the product of their time and its prevailing social conditions.

Although the shift today values system leaders, many people still hold fast to the assumptions underpinning the Great Man Theory, which influences and impacts their leadership behavior.

Scientific Management (1880)

Frederick Taylor created a theory of management that seeks to analyze and improve workflows. It was his attempt to apply science to the engineering process and to the process of managing people. Sometimes known as "Taylorism", scientific management was the first theory to integrate the process of work with the management practices needed to support the work.

Although scientific management faded out by the 1930s as more contemporary management practices were introduced for manufacturing, most of its themes are still an important part of industrial engineering, manufacturing, and management today.

Trait Theory (1910)

Trait theory is built upon the idea that leaders possess certain qualities or traits, and are different than other people. This led researchers to identify characteristic traits, with the assumption that some finite number could be quantified – and used as a filter to identify leaders.

The assumption that leaders have certain traits continues to be studied. Today's researchers have found correlations between certain personality characteristics (charisma, extroversion, conscientiousness, integrity, and achievement motivation) and leadership. With advanced research methodologies – including neuroscience – there is a renewed sense that defined traits can be used to identify potential leaders, explain leadership and play a part in its development.

Behavioral Theory (1950)

Stogdill's (1948) survey of 25 years of research concluded, "A person does not become a leader by virtue of the possession of some combination of traits." As a result, leadership research shifted away from traits (the internal factor) and towards behaviors – the external expression of leadership. The shift in thinking here was, "If we can't nail down the internal traits, we can look at the external behaviors of leaders."

As attention moved to behavioral expressions of leadership, the nature vs. nurture question became the focus. Can one learn to be a leader? With this new emphasis, and under the right conditions, leaders were seen to emerge as a product of their environment, as well as their nature. Two studies (Katz, Maccoby, Gurin and Floor in 1951, and Stogdill and Coons in 1957) identified two primary considerations: task-oriented vs. relationship-oriented leadership.

Contingency Theory (1967)

Contingency theories were developed to address the gap between traits, behaviors, and the context of leadership – other factors that impact leadership effectiveness. This research acknowledged that no single style of leadership was universally appropriate. Fiedler (1967, 1971), who is recognized as one of the trailblazers in this area, identified three managerial components: leader-member relations, task structure, and position power. Some contexts favored leaders who were task-oriented, and some favored those who were relationship-oriented. Hersey and Blanchard's situational leadership research (1969) suggested four leadership styles that were best used, and correlated effectively to four development styles. This common leadership framework is actively used today in many organizations.

Leader-Follower Theory (1970)

The role of followers was a natural extension of contingency theory and created a set of "Leader-Follower" theories. Robert Greenleaf's work on

Servant Leadership (1970) emphasized the choice of certain leaders to "serve" their followers, empowering them to live and work to their full potential. Research in servant leadership is ongoing and has shown to be a critical part to personal well-being as it relates to motivational values and self-development.

Graem and Uhl-Biewn (1995) furthered this research with the Leader-Member Exchange Theory. Here, high quality relations are characterized by trust and respect between leader and follower, while those of lower quality coincide with transactional and contractual obligations. High quality relations are empirically shown to produce better leader outcomes. Further research by Gerstner & Day (1997) and more currently Ilies, Nahrgang, and Morgeson (2007) continue to show that the relationship between the leader and follower is critical to leader effectiveness.

Transformational Leadership Theory (1978)

James MacGregor Burns (1978) first introduced the concept of transforming leadership. According to Burns, transforming leadership is a process in which "leaders and followers help each other to advance to a higher level of morale and motivation". Burns related to the difficulty in differentiation between management and leadership and claimed that the differences are in characteristics and behaviors. He established two concepts: "transforming leadership" and "transactional leadership". According to Burns, the transforming approach creates significant change in the life of people and organizations. It redesigns perceptions and values, and changes expectations and aspirations of employees. Unlike in the transactional approach, it is not based on a "give and take" relationship, but on the leader's personality, traits, ability to make a change through example, articulation of an energizing vision, and setting of challenging goals.

Another researcher, Bernard M. Bass (1985), extended the work by explaining the psychological mechanisms that underlie transforming and transactional leadership. Bass also used the term "transformational" instead of "transforming." His research helped explain how Transformational Leadership could be measured, as well as how it impacts follower motivation and performance.

System Leadership Theory (1990)

Although systems theory has been around since the 1800's, it was not until the 1990's that a systems approach to leadership was proposed. Here we see the integration of management and leadership and other sciences in the development of an organization and its employees. Like the human body, leadership requires numerous functions to integrate and interact in a way that produces a larger leadership outcome.

Peter Senge (1990) fathered the terms Systems Thinking and Organizational Development. Within Systems Leadership Theory, he developed the framework for a Learning Organization that more clearly defines leadership needs in the current interconnected world of work.

Although there are many popular models for leadership, many lack the foundation of behavioral science. Research continues in the area of leadership and management – most with the assumption of the organization as a living system, acknowledging the complexity of our current social, economic, and global cultures.

Just as Senge and others have noted, an individual, working alone, is unable to satisfy today's mix of personal, organizational, and global demands. Today, leaders at every level make choices to set aside personal ego and control, trust in their teams and talent, and better influence and direct others to achieve the desired needs of unique organizational systems.

"Leadership behaviors are all knit together,
much like the complex network of the human
brain.
There is an unbelievable interdependence
between them."

John H Zenger and Joseph Folkman

CHAPTER 2

A Better Leader Model

Multiple Points of View

Before we dive into LeadAbility, let's talk about the POV – or Point of View.

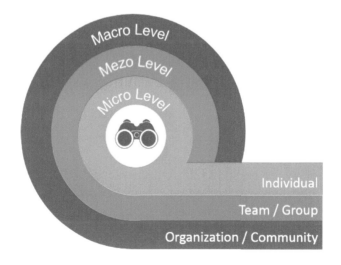

Leadership occurs on three levels and can be managed using Micro, Mezo, and Macro Points of View.

Micro

This level refers to the level of individuals. Here we are able to better understand ourselves, and in doing so, better understand others. Each of us has the opportunity to be better leaders, to develop and grow in our abilities to influence and impact the lives of others. This is our individual development and is critical to our understanding and application of the leadership principles discussed in this book. It is in this POV that we also realize that every team and every organization or community is just the sum of the individuals within it. As such, we need to always keep this Micro point of view in mind as we seek to influence and lead at any level. We will further explore this Point of View in Chapter 3: Personal LeadAbility.

Mezo

This level refers to the level of groups and teams. Leading groups and teams is challenging. We will not dive into the individual definition of groups vs. teams, other than to say that each are composed of two or more individuals working together. When these groups or teams work together, they not only experience leadership as individuals (Micro) but also as a unit (Mezo). As we seek to influence and impact others, it is important that we understand how the group / team level experiences leadership and what tools are available to help make team leadership more effective. We will further explore this Point of View in Chapter 4: Team LeadAbility.

Macro

This level refers to units consisting of smaller groups, organizations, and communities. In the field of management and leadership, this is often referred to as Organizational Leadership, although the practices used are not limited to just organizations. At this level, we must be aware that every Macro unit is made of teams, and ultimately is the sum of the individuals that identify with that unit. There are specific practices unique to this level, but they must be integrated with the practices of the Micro / Individual and the Mezo / Team levels. We will further explore this Point of View in Chapter 5: Organizational LeadAbility.

To be better leaders, we must build LeadAbility at each level. It is essential that we take into consideration each Point of View when reading each section of this book.

Becoming Better

We have created A Better Leader™ model. It's not necessarily the best leader model, nor is it the greatest leader model. We specifically chose the word "better" because we believe the following to be true:

- EVERYONE has the potential to be A Better Leader.
- Better Leaders integrate both Leadership and Management mindsets.
- Better Leaders demonstrate their Leadership as Choices and Abilities.
- Better Leaders look to make a positive difference in the lives of those around them.

By using the word "Better", we are making the commitment to everyone that leadership development is not about reaching a specific level or role, but rather an ongoing challenge to always grow, develop, and become better leaders in both our personal and professional lives.

By using the word "Better", we recognize that leadership already exists in our teams, organizations, families, and community groups. However, we believe that everyone has the potential to continue to grow and develop – to become better leaders. In fact, we will look to leaders that already have mastery in an area of leadership to mentor and coach those that are not as experienced in their leadership.

It is vitally important that all team members know that they are Leaders. EVERY person, regardless of their title or role, has the potential to positively influence others and to provide needed direction and insight as we work together to achieve a mission and vision, be it personal or professional.

It is also our desire to equip, empower, encourage, and enable leadership that transcends ourselves. By growing and developing our leadership at work, we will also build skills and abilities that we can take into our personal lives – leading in our families, in our communities, and making a difference in the world we live in.

Six Leadership Choices

Our most powerful human characteristic is our ability to choose how we will think, feel, and behave in any given situation. Although there are hundreds of behavioral sets, competencies, and traits that are used to evaluate someone's leadership and management, we believe there are Six Leadership Choices that form the foundation of being a better leader at work, in our communities, and in our homes.

Each Leadership Choice represents many different behaviors that impact our influence at the micro (individual), mezo (team/group), and macro (organization/community) levels. We have specifically used the term "Choice" so as not to fall into the "natural born leader" syndrome. Each of us is born with the freedom to choose – and it is in this freedom where we choose to better positively influence the behaviors of others and provide needed direction to achieve our desired results.

Our leadership effectiveness is not ruled by situations, procedures, or practices. We make thousands of choices every day that impact our LeadAbility. The following six Leadership Choices are best practices that are common to every leader at every level.

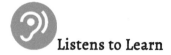

Listens to Learn

Listening is the foundation for A Better Leader. How we demonstrate our understanding of what people say determines whether they feel valued and heard. Listening to understand is different than listening to hear. Often, we spend our time in conversation focused on what we will say next, rather than seeking to understand not only what the other person is saying, but also how they are communicating with us.

Developing and fostering better communication skills is a choice. It requires intention, practice, and discipline. Good communication begins with understanding diverse communication styles, core convictions, and problem-solving skills. Learning how to leverage these effectively will help build and maintain better relationships personally and professionally.

Choosing a mindset of problem-solving and a desire to resolve conflict is critical to becoming a Better Leader. Looking for opportunities to learn from others, personally and professionally, help us to leverage wisdom and further expand our own knowledge and experience.

Builds Trust

Without trust, there is no relationship. Success in both our personal and professional lives is built upon relationships. Better Leaders take the time to consider how people perceive them and how they can improve the way they relate to others. Trust takes time to build, can be destroyed in an instant, and takes even longer to rebuild once broken.

Being a champion of others' well-being and choosing to collaborate in decision-making are key ways to build trust. Choosing to always do what you say you will do is the simplest way to build trust, and sometimes small changes can make big strides forward in becoming a trusted advisor and friend.

Building, developing, and working effectively in teams is crucial to accomplishing goals, in life and in work. A Better Leader's ability to understand how teams work and how they evolve over time plays an important part in fostering a team culture that maximizes collaboration and communication, creating a positive and inclusive experience for others.

 Seeks the Better

Seeing the possible instead of the impossible is a critical choice in leadership. The saying says, "what we seek, we find" because if we focus on only what is lacking or what is not happening, we lose sight of the inspiring future we are seeking to build in our workplaces and communities. Seeking the Better isn't ignoring the negative, but rather placing the negative in context of the possibilities to learn, grow, and develop ourselves and others.

All around us are people from various cultures, backgrounds, countries, lifestyles, generations, and beliefs. Being inclusive means that we choose to treat every person with dignity, compassion, integrity, and respect simply because they breathe and we value their input and insights. Bridging cultural gaps and increasing a sense of common vision and purpose builds stronger teams and personal relationships.

Significant research has been conducted on the link between well-being and gratitude. Our choice to be thankful, appreciating what is good in ourselves and others, and seeking to find the truth and benefit in any situation, creates psychological safety for both ourselves and for others. Better Leaders seek to find what others are doing right, rather than trying to catch others doing wrong.

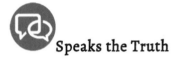 Speaks the Truth

The choice to analyze situations in a clear, objective, and unbiased way is a hallmark of A Better Leader. Examining facts, obtaining information, probing for answers, and a willingness to be appropriately transparent are all prerequisites to speaking the truth.

Better Leaders expand their thinking beyond their own limited knowledge, understanding, beliefs, and experiences to seek out perspectives that may differ from their own. Speaking the truth should always be done with dignity, compassion, integrity, and respect and is not only reserved for when giving feedback or correction. Speaking the truth enables us to share our appreciation for others' viewpoints that may not align with our own.

Coaching others requires us to clearly set expectations and hold ourselves and others accountable to what has been agreed upon. Managing conflict and disagreements are a reality for any leader. Avoiding conversations that are unpleasant or uncomfortable isn't an option for A Better Leader. Whether in our personal or professional relationships, effective coaching and conflict resolution are skills we need in speaking truth.

 Thinks then Acts

Too often decisions are made in haste and based on emotion and personal assumptions. Better leaders seek to think BEFORE they act in given situations. When leaders take the time to involve the right people, think through the impacts and issues from multiple perspectives and use a rational approach to making a decision, they increase the likelihood of achieving their desired results.

Thinking strategically and thinking critically are essential to making sound decisions. These ways of thinking build credibility and help earn the trust of those you lead. Being able to create and communicate the vision or mission of an organization, community, team, or individual initiative is as important as learning how to act and react so that daily decisions are realistic and measurably aligned with the strategy you present.

 Walks the Talk

One of the most common Choices that others attribute to Leadership is "Walking the Talk". We admire those that have charisma and can create and communicate a compelling vision – but leaders lose their credibility when they don't do what they say they are going to do. Even worse, they break our trust when their behaviors are not aligned with the beliefs they preach to others. Many communities and organizations have suffered harm when their leaders chose to do something in contradiction to what they said they believed, or broke the promises made on how they behaved.

You may be asking why we chose to present "Walks the Talk" as the last Leadership Choice. Well, it's because the other five Leadership Choices, when communicated to others as a Leadership Model, become "the Talk" which we then need to "Walk". Without having a defined set of expectations, beliefs, or ideals, it's impossible to deliver results and be accountable. Many leaders choose to be ambiguous or vague in their definition of leadership or in the behaviors they expect of themselves or others, thus creating confusion and credibility issues for those they seek to influence and lead.

To be a Better Leader, we must make the choice to Listen to Learn, Build Trust, Seek the Better, Speak the Truth, Think then Act, and finally, Walk the Talk to align with our Leadership Choices.

The Seventh Choice

You may be asking, what do I do if I have 20 years of leadership experience, have taken multiple leadership assessments, participated in many leadership development workshops and achieved a level of "mastery" in each of the Six Leadership Choices? Great question!

If you find yourself in this situation, the challenge then is to fulfill The Seventh Choice, which is to Selflessly Serve. It is in service to others and to our communities that human beings find their greatest Joy. As we have grown beyond our own self-awareness and self-actualization, there is a human drive to give back, to invest in others and, in doing so, leave a legacy that is built on service rather than one built solely on self-interest.

Selflessly Lead

If there is a single characteristic that reflects a servant-leader, it is the DESIRE to serve. It is not a specific skill or ability, but rather an internal desire and choice to put others first.

Robert K. Greenleaf coined the term "servant-leader" and "servant leadership" in 1970 with the publication of his essay "The Servant Leader." Greenleaf defined the servant-leader as follows:

> "The servant-leader is servant first... It begins with the natural feeling that one wants to serve, to serve first. Then conscious choice brings one to aspire to lead. That person is sharply different from one who is leader first, perhaps because of the need to assuage an unusual power drive or to acquire material possessions... The leader-first and the servant-first are two extreme types. Between them there are shadings and blends that are part of the infinite variety of human nature. The difference manifests itself in the care taken by the servant-first leader to make sure that other people's highest priority needs are being served."

People are often confused with the term "service". They assume that it means that the leader is subservient and taking direction on what to do, when to do it, and how to do it from their employees. Built into this assumption is an incorrect belief that one cannot lead and serve at the same time.

As you will notice in other areas of this book, we start with a belief in the "AND" instead of "OR" when approaching a concept. As such, we believe, and it is supported by behavioral science, that people can both Lead and Serve at the same time, thus creating the choice to adapt to a mindset of Servant-Leadership.

When we look at any organization or group, we often see a pyramid shape. At the top are the Executives, below them are the management, and below them are the frontline employees. All the power seems to rest at the top of the organization, and everyone is responsible and reactive to the position that is higher on the totem pole. Top down leadership creates the skill set of "managing-up" in the organization, drawing focus away from customers. The focus on the level above repurposes energy to be spent moving up the chain with people getting promotions based on their upward-influencing skills. As a result, attention is not focused on the customers, solutions, and frontline employees – diminishing customer satisfaction and employee morale.

Being responsible and responsive allows servant leaders to maintain their accountability to achieving results while building effective relationships with those they serve. Selflessly serving doesn't mean that a manager gives up decision-making or accountability for their teams. Instead, having set the direction and expectations, the servant leader shifts into a role of helping employees accomplish goals, solve problems, and achieve the desired results.

As such, being a servant leader is a choice – it isn't a technique, characteristic, or set of traits. It is a choice in the way one chooses to behave and a mindset that is adopted over the longer term. If you believe you have a level of mastery in the Six Leadership Choices, you now have an opportunity to shift your mindset and selflessly serve those you lead.

CHAPTER 3

Personal LeadAbility

A Question of Character

Most leadership models have a center Core that refers to the organization's Mission, Vision, and Core Values. As we believe LeadAbility should be developed both personally and professionally, the core of A Better Leader™ is our Character.

Character refers to those values and goals that make us who we are. I heard a leader once say that "Character is who you are when no one is looking."

Organizationally, we express those values and goals in a set of mission and vision statements and organizational values. Personally, it refers to our individual set of values, motivations, beliefs, and the foundations of our identity.

As individuals, it is near impossible to set a definition that encompasses all of humanity's uniqueness and diversity. Research in the areas of character and character development have identified four components that help us to better understand the type of Character we believe makes the best team members and leaders. They are:

- **Helpful:** I am focused on helping others and creating movement forward.

- **Honest:** I value truth and make data-driven decisions.

- **Humble:** I realize that I am not the center of importance and that I can be wrong.

- **Hungry:** I strive for excellence in all I do and seek to always be better.

When we look to hire, promote, reward, and recognize leaders in our organization, we will be looking at their Character, in addition to their demonstrated Choices and Abilities. When we look to connect with others in our communities to accomplish desired results, we will also be looking at how they demonstrate these four components of Character.

A Dozen LeadAbilities™

LeadAbility is an Ability. It is a competency or capability that can be developed, grown, and mastered. By understanding how we experience leadership, we gain confidence and feel better equipped in our ability to influence and provide direction. By also understanding how others experience leadership, we can improve our relationships and help our teams and organizations more effectively reach results.

For each Leadership Choice, we have specific abilities that we can choose to develop on an individual basis. Although there are hundreds of abilities associated with Leadership, we have chosen twelve LeadAbilities that increase our effectiveness in becoming A Better Leader.

Each of the LeadAbilities begins with the word "to" because they require certain behaviors to be demonstrated. Having confidence in the ability to do something is of little value unless you can demonstrate the ability and put it into practical experience. For each of the LeadAbilities, we include key actions that can be used to assess your development level in each of the LeadAbilities. We talk more about development levels in Chapter 5.

The list of actions below is just a starting point, as there are hundreds of possible actions that can be chosen to demonstrate each of the 12 LeadAbilities.

Listens to Learn

A Leader that chooses to Listen to Learn will demonstrate the following LeadAbilities:

To Communicate

- Expressing thoughts, feelings, and ideas in a clear and compelling manner in both individual and group situations.

- Conveying information and ideas in ways that seeks to build connection and adapts messaging to build better understanding.

- Facilitating discussions in a way that considers each person's viewpoint and communication needs.

To Problem Solve

- Identifying and understanding issues, problems, and opportunities.

- Soliciting feedback and data from different sources before drawing conclusions.

- Taking action that aligns with the mission, vision, and values of the organization.

Builds Trust

A Leader that chooses to Build Trust will demonstrate the following LeadAbilities:

To Champion

- Championing and clearly communicating the culture, mission, vision, and values of the organization.

- Helping others understand what makes us unique and keeping our values at the forefront of all decision-making.

- Championing new initiatives, identifying your role in the change process and creating opportunities for others to learn, practice and experience new ideas.

To Collaborate

- Using appropriate methods and interpersonal styles to develop, motivate, and guide others toward successful outcomes.

- Building effective relationships with others to work collaboratively in meeting organizational goals and objectives.

- Building and promoting teamwork among groups; discouraging "us vs them" thinking by establishing and reinforcing shared values and norms.

 Seeks the Better

A Leader that chooses to Seek the Better will demonstrate the following LeadAbilities:

To Include

- Encouraging others to develop and grow in their professional and personal development.

- Championing new ideas, inclusivity, and innovative approaches to meet team and organizational needs.

- Creating an environment in which people from diverse backgrounds and beliefs feel valued, heard, and given the opportunity to contribute.

To Develop

- Identifying required capabilities and skills needed to be most effective in the role and use data to identify top-priorities in development.

- Putting new knowledge to practical use on the job, learning new skills, and taking on challenging assignments to continuously grow and develop.

- Reinforcing the value of development experiences, creating an effective learning environment.

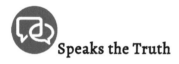 **Speaks the Truth**

A Leader that chooses to Speak the Truth will demonstrate the following LeadAbilities:

To Coach

- Setting clear expectations of desired results.

- Planning and supporting the development of skills and abilities for the purpose of fulfilling current or future responsibilities.

- Giving both positive and developmental feedback in a timely manner with dignity, compassion, understanding, and respect.

To Be Transparent

- Encouraging open exchange for information and viewpoints, expressing reactions and opinions without intimidating others.

- Communicating data accurately to reflect business priorities and needs.

- Sharing (as appropriate) information needed by others to achieve individual, group, and organizational results.

Thinks then Acts

A Leader that chooses to Think then Act will demonstrate the following LeadAbilities:

To Think Strategically

- Demonstrating the ability to "Connect the Dots" seeing what others often miss.

- Establishing and committing to long-range course of action, while understanding short-term impacts of decisions on people, resources, and business results.

- Ensuring initiatives and priorities are integrated with one another and aligned with the mission, vision, values, and priorities of the organization.

To Think Critically

- Comparing data from different sources to draw conclusions and provide solutions.

- Taking action that is consistent with available facts, constraints, resources, and business goals.

- Thinking critically and realistically about outcomes and results of decisions being made.

 Walks the Talk

A Leader that chooses to Walk the Talk will demonstrate the following LeadAbilities:

To Deliver Results

- Translating the organization mission, vision, and values into day-to-day activities and outcomes.

- Using measurement methods to monitor accurate progress toward goals and tenaciously working to exceed those goals with integrity and excellence.

- Handling multiple demands and competing priorities, making efficient use of time to consistently maintain a high standard of performance.

To Be Accountable

- Maintaining responsibility, purpose, and accountability for our actions and behaviors.

- Demonstrating awareness of how choices impact credibility and outcomes.

- Holding self accountable before holding others accountable for choices.

We all can all become better leaders. Everyone, regardless of their experience, education, and expertise, have the opportunity to grow and develop in their LeadAbility and demonstrate a level of development in each of the LeadAbilities. Further discussion on how to assess development levels is discussed in the next chapter.

Effectiveness and Personal LeadAbility

Effective Conversations (CARE)

Over the last 20 years, I have experienced all sorts of training to help make conversations more effective. Unfortunately, each model or theory has been set to apply to only one circumstance. There is the STAR model for interviews, the SBI model for difficult conversations, and many others. Being a more simple person, I prefer to have one tool that can apply to many different situations, thereby providing a higher level of mastery in the tool.

As such, I believe the CARE acronym is the best tool for increasing the effectiveness of conversations. These conversations can be helpful during the interview process, as part of a development discussion, or in a difficult discussion that requires a desired change in behavior. If we can master the CARE method of conversation, we not only have a strong tool but also a tool that seeks to have both parties be in the best possible position to build effective relationships.

Before going through each step in a CARE conversation, we must start with the premise of positive intent. Any tool, be it a hammer or a spoon, can be used for the good of others or used for destruction. The tool itself is neither good or bad, but the impact of its use can be positive or negative. Therefore, when using the CARE method of effective conversations, we must start with the ultimate desire of building more effective relationships, whether at work or in life.

Context

One of the more challenging aspects of any conversation is having one person start in the middle of a thought, and the other person is left in a place of wonder. Whether or not you are giving appreciative feedback or performance feedback, the context is the first thing we must bring to the table of conversation. Context is especially important when there is a time delay from the action being referenced and the onset of the conversation.

For example, I have entered into discussions with others where they have assumed I already know what they have been thinking about before I entered the room. As they jump in and begin sharing what they need from me, I have to pause and awkwardly ask, "what are you talking about?" By starting with Context, we bring all members of the conversation to the same starting point.

Actions

Once Context has been established, we need to present the specific actions we are looking to discuss. This stage is about data, facts, and specific behaviors – this is NOT a step of emotions or feelings. The more objective and specific we can be, the more effective the overall conversation will become. When you are having appreciative conversations, the actions and behaviors are ones you are seeking to empower and encourage. When you are having an interview conversation, the actions and behaviors are ones you are looking to provide credibility and experience. When you are having a performance discussion, the actions and behaviors are ones you are looking to coach or redirect into higher performance. Regardless of the context, the actions need to be observable actions and behaviors.

Often individuals having difficult conversations are tempted to use the phrase "I think you meant" or "You intended to" – both of which indicate an ability to read the other person's mind. This is obviously not objective nor based on actions and behaviors. Be careful not to throw your own bias or opinion when sharing the actions and behaviors being discussed.

Results

Once you have set the stage with context, shone the light on specific actions and behaviors, it's time to share the impact the actions and behaviors had in the situation being discussed. If this is an appreciative discussion, the impact may be an increased in sales, or the decrease in service calls. If this is a performance discussion, the impact may be the decrease in sales, or the increase in service calls.

Because we have started with Context, the person has a frame of reference. The actions and behaviors allow the person to know exactly what it is that they did that has led to this conversation. The sharing of results shows the person the impact – positive, neutral, or negative – that their actions have had on the situation. If you can not articulate the results, you should not be discussing the behaviors. Many times behaviors will be brought up and the only result is "I just don't like it". For most relationships, this answer is neither effective nor appreciated.

<u>E</u>xpectations

Context, Actions, and Results have now been shared. It is important to close the statement with establishing clear expectations to move forward. In an appreciative discussion, we would be looking for those behaviors to continue and maybe increase. In a performance discussion, we would be looking for those behaviors to change into specific desired behaviors. The largest contributor to distrust in any relationship or team is the failure to provide clear expectations.

Often I get asked to provide an example of how the CARE model can be used in real life, so here are a few:

Appreciative – At the employee event on Saturday (Context) you arrived early and helped set up tables and chairs (Action), resulting in us being able to start the event on time (Result). I appreciate you going above and beyond in this situation and encourage you to continue taking initiative that helps us reach our event goals (Expectations).

Performance – At the employee event on Saturday (Context) you arrived after your call time (Action) resulting in others having to do the jobs assigned to you, specifically setting up tables and chairs (Result). As part of the team, it is expected that each member will be on time to each event and be ready to do the work that is assigned to them (Expectations).

Interview– We often do large events (Context), please tell me what events experience you have (Actions) and how you contributed to the event goals and objectives (Results). Also share how your event experience aligns with event requirements for this role (Expectations).

Using the CARE model for effective communication is not something you can do "on the fly" but rather requires pre-thought and practice. When we are purposeful in planning for effective conversations, we set ourselves, and others, on a path of success. When we jump in with emotion and lack of preparation, we damage our credibility and diminish potential effectiveness. Effective conversations are a learned skill and an ability we can grow and develop as we seek to build more effective relationships in our personal and professional lives.

Effectiveness Study

The two most significant choices we have each day are how we spend our money and how we spend our time. Imagine, that you were given $86,400 each day that you were required to spend in any way you wanted, however, after the 24 hours were up, you had to give back any of the unspent funds. For most people, this would become a priority to manage and maximize so as not to lose out on any of the funds being returned.

Well, in many ways, we have this situation each day. We are given 86,400 seconds each day and we get to choose how to spend them. Once the day is done, our time is gone and we no longer have access to it. So the question really is, "Do you spend your time with the same focus and energy you would if each second was representing a dollar in your bank account?".

Like most people, chances are you waste time in areas and things you should not be doing. Some areas may represent more of a problem than others. If we are to improve the effective management of ourselves and our time, we must determine our time wasters and start working on them. Why? Because a problem that has not been identified cannot be corrected.

The Insight-Based Learning Methodology is a cognitive-behavioral approach to looking at situations, collecting information, gaining insight from the data, and making a choice to create an action plan that will positively impact your situation.

I encourage you to use the Insight-Based Learning Methodology as part of your Effectiveness Study. There are three steps to this process.

Information – Data Collection

The first step is to collect your data. I have found that 30-minute increments are the most powerful to document what was done. Set a quiet timer for every 30 minutes and, when the time is up, write down a quick set of bullet points on what you did in that time. Then do it again, and again, and again until your log is completed. During the Data Collection, you are not to filter or try to evaluate your data. You are simply to record the data – the actions and behaviors you have demonstrated. Once your time log is complete, then you can move to the next step, which is Insights / Analysis.

To use your time more effectively, you must first discover what you actually do with your time. The only tool I have found to be useful in this area is a time log. Having a time log for **one week** (7 days) will document how you spend your time, from the moment you wake to the moment you sleep. This will paint a picture of how you make use of your days. After completing the time log, it is encouraged to journal your Insights.

Insight – Analysis

Having completed your time log, it is now time to look at the data. As you spread your time logs out in front of you, what patterns of behavior to you see? What types of activities did you spend the most of your time doing? Where were your discoveries? Did you have any disappointments? And what insights can you draw from the reviewing of your own personal data?

We spend most of our time on those things that are most important to us. What does your time log say about what you value most in your life? Does this align with what you believe is most important to you?

Impact – Action Plan

Having Information and Insight are excellent disciplines, however, without a choice to act, there will be no Impact. My favorite saying is "Education without Application is just Useless Information." To maximize effectiveness, we must go beyond the "Ah-Ha" and seek to make an Impact with this new Information and Insight. One of the best ways to do so, is to write Impact Statements. These statements simply begin with, I will...

One of the foundations of trust is credibility – that we do what we say we will do. Having Impact Statements provides the "what we say we will do" and sets clear expectations as to what set of actions and behaviors that will move us forward in achieving our goals and objectives.

Some have asked why I recommend 7 consecutive days for a time log – be it personal or professional. The primary reason is that, as human beings, we will subconsciously adapt our behaviors for the first couple of days in an attempt to make ourselves look good. However, it is difficult to carry on this "halo-effect" for the entire week. For those that really want a challenge, collect your data for 2 consecutive weeks. This process also works with Team Effectiveness and Family Effectiveness – try doing this exercise with your team or family to see what Insights you can gain from how you use your time.

CHAPTER 4

Team LeadAbility

It's the Manager

One of Gallup's most significant discoveries is that the manager or team leader alone accounts for over 70% of the variance in team engagement. As such, the single most important component of successful teams is the quality of the person leading them.

One of the primary concerns of any organization is that of employee performance. A raft of studies over the last 90 years has found that leadership management behavior is a primary predictor of performance of employees. Indeed, many studies, particularly around service industry organizations, have gone as far as to say that the success of the organization is largely dependent on its managers and leaders. The main reason for this statement is that it is the knowledge, attitudes, emotional capability, skills, and behavior of the leaders that have the main influence on employees' own emotions, behaviors, thinking, and attitudes.

Furthermore, Gallup found that an awareness of a team's abilities is far more predictive of the team's success than the composition of the team's abilities. As such, team LeadAbility requires a clear understanding of each team member's Communication Style and their level of skill development in each of the specific skills needed by the team.

Gallup has also found that only 21% of employees strongly agree that their organization is committed to building the abilities of each employee. Prior to evaluating levels of skill and how to maximize development, team leaders need to have a clear idea of the desired results and what skills are needed for the team to achieve the vision being set by the team leader.

Levels of Skill Development

A people manager, whether a team lead, functional manager or executive, needs to understand that their role is critical to the organization's success. Understanding the level of skills development is critical for any leader. For each level we have three points of view – the "needed," the "now", and the "next".

The Needed

We must start with understanding what skills are needed for the role, team, or organization to reach our desired goals. It is important to note the essential nature of starting with reviewing the role first, then the individuals within that role. Many a discrimination lawsuit has been won because leaders made decisions based on the person prior to reviewing the needs of the role and the organization.

For each set of skills needed for a role, we need to also determine the level of skill needed to reach our desired results. The combination of needed skills and needed levels of those skills provide us the blueprint for how to fill that role with a person that is ready and capable to be successful in the role. For example, the role of trainer will need to have a much higher level of skill in the area of "presenting information" than someone working in operations. Having these expectations set prior to hiring or promoting help establish data-driven decisions and create clear understanding with everyone involved in the process.

The Now

Whether we have someone already in a role, or an individual is being considered for the role, we must look at what their skill levels are in the "now". Having set clear expectations with the needed skill set and the needed level of skills required, it is the leader's responsibility to discuss skill levels with the individual.

For those being considered for a role, there should be a detailed job description and a skills profile that the individuals use to determine if they are a match for the role they are seeking. Often, Human Resource functions within an organization will provide tools and training for interviewing to equip hiring managers with the skills needed to make effective hiring decisions.

The Next

Having a detailed job description and skills profile for each role not only helps in hiring, but also helps in promotions and succession planning. Research shows that a focus on hiring from within the organization helps to maintain engagement as individuals see opportunities to grow and develop into new roles instead of having to leave the organization to move forward in their careers.

When discussing succession or promotion, we must again start with the role, not the person. So often individuals get promoted into roles that they are not qualified for simply because they have been with the organization for a number of years. Time in a role does not guarantee an individual is ready, or wanting, the next level of responsibility.

Having the expectations for each role clearly articulated, organizations can start from a place of equality and choose to evaluate based on the skills data of an individual in comparison with the roles being reviewed for succession candidates. Knowing that candidates for succession may not be "ready now" means that we need to discuss what are the skills and experience gaps to get them effectively prepared for "the next" role. We discuss Talent Planning in more detail in Chapter 7.

Skill Level Model

Having a standard for Skill Levels creates a common language and clarity of expectations. It is important to note that each skill has two components – the experience using the skill and the consistency of excellence when demonstrating the skill. Just because I have 20 years' experience in driving does not necessarily mean I am a good driver. I will need to consistently demonstrate my ability to drive as well.

Using the example earlier, instead of saying the trainer needs "more" presentation skills than someone working in an operational role, we have the following five levels we can use instead.

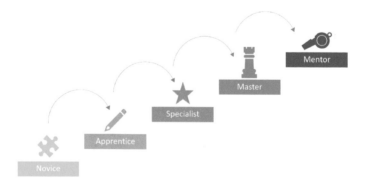

- **Novice.** Individuals have an interest in the needed skill set but no practical experience or opportunities to demonstrate the skills successfully.

- **Apprentice.** Individuals have some experience with varied levels of consistency in their application of the needed skills.

- **Specialist (Journeyman).** Individuals have solid experience and consistently deliver a level of proficiency in the needed skills.

- **Master (Expert).** Individuals have advanced level of experience and consistently exceed the level of proficiency in the needed skills.

- **Mentor (Servant).** Individuals have an advanced level of experience and are seen as the standard of excellence for that skill set, often resulting in the individual mentoring and coaching others to grow and develop that needed skills.

It is important to note that we use these Skill Levels for a set of skills, not when referring to a person. A role will have many skill sets needed. Therefore, a person may have different levels in their overall skill proficiency. Having a list of the skills needed for the role (skills profile) makes the process of evaluating skill level significantly more effective.

It is important that we do not fall to the temptation to categorize a Person such as "Pat is a Master." Instead we would refer to Pat as a "Professional with Mastery in presentation skills and a Specialist level in accounting, and an Apprentice level of skills in computers." This would lead us to believe that Pat would be a good candidate for an Accounting Trainer role, however, may not be a best fit for a Computer Trainer role.

Ideally, if Pat has a Mastery level in presentation skills, and we can further develop the skill sets needed for computers, we could place Pat on a development plan to move the computer skills from an Apprentice level to a Specialist level. If a leader sees potential in the individual to grow and develop in a skill set, a development plan is an excellent way to invest in talent we already have and increase organizational readiness and employee engagement. We discuss this further in Chapter 7.

Three Tools for Team Effectiveness

In our book AdaptAbility, we shared Google's research on building Team Effectiveness. An area of struggle in team leadership is often in the area of Structure and Clarity.

People often leave jobs because they lack a real understanding of what is expected of them, and how their job responsibilities impact the overall mission and vision of the organization. This is the same for teams. Clear roles and responsibilities, job expectations, expected process to be followed, and the consequences of performance are important to team effectiveness.

There are three tools that will help you personally and professionally as you seek to increase effectiveness. Goals are critical and can be set at the individual or group level and should be "SMART". Priority management needs to be simple and an ongoing process. Decision-making processes must be clearly understood and well documented.

SMART Goals

Goal setting is one of the most effective and yet least used tools for achieving goals. Whether in our personal lives or in our workplaces, having well-articulated goals is critical for our effectiveness. Many years ago, I was introduced to the concept of SMART goals. Using this simple acronym has been incredibly helpful in keeping my goals **S**pecific, **M**easurable, **A**ttainable, **R**elevant, and **T**imely.

Specific   Measurable   Attainable   Relevant   Timed

Specific

When setting a goal, be specific about what you want to accomplish. Think about this as the mission statement that includes the popular 'W' questions:

- **Who.** Consider who needs to be involved to achieve the goal (this is especially important when you're working on a group project).

- **What**. Think about exactly what you are trying to accomplish and don't be afraid to get very detailed.

- **When**. You'll get more specific about this question under the "time-bound" section of defining SMART goals, but you should at least set a timeframe.

- **Where**. This question may not always apply, especially if you're setting personal goals, but if there's a location or relevant event, identify it here.

- **Why**. What is the reason for the goal? Goals should be purposeful and have a clearly defined reason why they are a priority given other choices you make with your time and energy.

Measurable

What metrics are you going to use to determine if you meet the goal? This makes a goal more tangible because it provides a way to measure progress. If it's a project that's going to take a few months to complete, then set some milestones by considering specific tasks to accomplish. Milestones are a series of steps along the way that when added up will result in the completion of your main goal.

There should be a source of information to measure or determine whether a goal has been achieved. Sometimes measurement is difficult to identify the most relevant and feasible data sources and collection methods. As such, knowing what data you need to confirm your measures is better to know in the planning stage of any goal or project.

Often a direct measurement source is not immediately feasible for a given goal. In this case, try to articulate what success looks like for your goal and how you would be able to determine if your goal was successfully completed or not.

Attainable

A goal that is not attainable isn't worth the paper it's printed on. When creating SMART goals, we need to ask if the goal is within our capability and capacity to achieve. Capability refers to the skills and abilities one needs to meet the expectations. Capacity refers to the bandwidth and the resources (time, energy, budget) to meet expectations. Understanding what resources your goal requires, and making sure the resources are available and appropriately attainable, must also be considered when creating a SMART goal.

Relevant

A goal should be relevant and results-oriented. It represents a worthwhile objective that integrates into a larger priority, plan, or initiative. The goal must be consistent with other goals and fit into your longer-term planning (e.g. budget and time) and the efforts required to complete the goal must be within the control of the person being held accountable to achieve it.

Include results-oriented in this area of SMART goals. The goal should be written in a way that clearly shows what the end results will be, or the results of each milestone. Results and relevance partner with the measures and metrics for goal completion as well as whether the goal is attainable.

Timed

Anyone can set goals, but if it lacks realistic timing, chances are you're not going to succeed.

Providing a target date for deliverables is imperative. Ask specific questions about the goal deadline and what can be accomplished within the expected timeframe.

Once there is specific, measurable, attainable, and relevant information, the final step is providing a timeline for the goal to be accomplished. Time is often considered a measure, however, providing time constraints also creates a sense of urgency.

Having goals laid out in the SMART format provides a personal level of clarity, but also provides a clear understanding for others as to what is expected. A misunderstanding on goals will drive a team to distrust and fall short of expectations. Having SMART goals at every level (individual, group, or organization) is highly recommended.

Priority Matrix

No matter how engaged, invested, and detail-oriented you may be, it's impossible to execute every task with the same level of attention—it's also not necessary.

Setting a priority list or mapping out a priority chart takes advantage of your brain's hard wiring ability to focus on the most important tasks at hand. Psychologists call this selective attention – the brain's natural tendency of filtering out unnecessary information, as it is constantly taking in and working through information. This type of focus is goal-oriented and creates brain functioning that is based on prior experiences and current conditions.

We often have misunderstanding on what should be our focus and our priorities – either as an individual or as a team member. Having a clear understanding of priorities is critical for any level of effectiveness in work and life. The process is simple:

1. Identify all the projects, tasks, or items that are being done, or that will need to be done.
2. Determine the level of importance (high / low) and urgency (high / low).
3. Place the items on a Priority Matrix like the one shown on the facing page.

It is important to keep the "level" of item similar. For example, if you are prioritizing projects, all the items on the matrix should be projects. If you are looking at your daily tasks, all of the items on the matrix should be tasks you perform as part of your daily work.

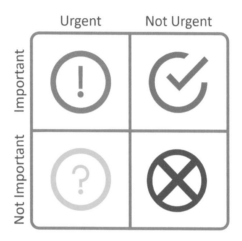

Important and Urgent

In Quadrant 1 we see the items that are both important and urgent. These are necessities and must be managed with the utmost attention. Crisis, emergency, and deadline are often words associated with items that fall in this quadrant. We have used the red icon with the exclamation point purposefully. Items in this quadrant take priority and override any other priorities on the matrix and must be completed.

Important and Not Urgent

In Quadrant 2 we see items that are important but not urgent. This includes items for day-to-day operations that need preparation and planning. We use a checkmark symbol, as these items are often routine and just need to be accomplished within the expected timelines. Be careful not to let items "rest" in this quadrant until they become urgent. Priority management challenges us to effectively plan and perform well on items in Quadrants 1 and 2, often simultaneously.

Urgent but Not Important

In Quadrant 3 we see items that are determined to be urgent but not important. I call these the "Great Deceivers", as many times they are not nearly as urgent as we think. Here we often have tasks and responsibilities that may belong to others, or are priorities that have been set by someone else without your involvement. Their lack of planning becomes your urgent, but not important, priority. We use yellow purposefully as these tasks can take up more time and energy while not helping achieve your goals and objectives. Be wary and be willing to ask questions, most importantly "Why is this urgent?" and then determine if the item needs to move up to Quadrant 1.

Neither Urgent nor Important

In Quadrant 4 we see items that are determined to be neither urgent nor important. Based on that definition, we need to question if they should be on a list of priorities at all. Items in this box are what I call the "Great Distractors." They include things we might enjoy doing, yet only serve as a distraction from the items or task we need to be doing. Social media is a key contributor to this box! Checking Facebook, twitter, and Instagram are neither urgent nor important for most people while at work. However, so much time and energy is taken in checking the apps and responding to and monitoring the multiple "conversations" involved.

One of the best practices in determining effectiveness is conducting a time study. In short, you write down all the things you are working on within each 30 or 60-minute period at the end of that period. For example, at 10 am I would look back at what I actually did in the last hour and write down some bullets. Do this for a week and, after collecting your data, look at the trends and see what insights you can gain on how you manage your priorities – at work and at home. Once we have a more realistic idea of what we actually do, we can more effectively plan and make decisions on how we prioritize.

RAPID Decision Making

Decision-making is an important foundation for any organization, regardless of its size and complexity. Everyone makes decisions every day that impact our effectiveness on different levels – individual, group, and organizational. As making decisions can be difficult and leads to overthinking, the management consulting firm Bain & Company created a tool to help streamline the decision-making process.

Each letter in RAPID reflects a role and responsibility within a decision, especially those decisions that impact more than one person – which is most of our decisions these days. The process is simple. Following the descriptions below, identify who needs to be involved in the decision making and what type of interactions they will need. For example, only one person can have the "D" for Decide as part of their role. Determining who that person is and gaining agreement that they ultimately have the final decision is an important discussion to have on any project or task.

Recommend   Agree   Perform   Input   Decide

Recommend

Individuals or groups in this category are responsible for making the recommendations. This group gathers data and analyzes the relevant facts gained from those with Input (I) and provides recommendations, solutions, and options to the person who will make the final Decision (D). Most of the work in the decision-making process happens with this group. In fact, Bain & Company states that 80% of work happens here.

Agree

Individuals and groups in this category are responsible for creating and maintaining agreement with the decision being made. They are actively engaged with the Recommendations (R) as those with Agree (A) must be willing and able to fully support the decision being made. Typically, individuals or groups in this category are limited to legal, finance, regulatory compliance, quality, and others that have a strong influence on the result of the decision.

Perform

Individuals or groups in this category are responsible for executing the decision once it is made. They are accountable for making the decision happen and translating the decision from idea to implementation. It is wise to have those responsible for execution of a decision also have Input (I) into the decision process.

Input

Individuals or groups in this category provide input, valuable expertise, and information. This information is usually needed by those categorized as Recommend. People in this category need to be consulted before any decision can be made.

Decide

This single individual makes the final decision and has the authority to commit resources towards the achievement of the task or project. They are the single point of accountability and therefore, there can only be one Decide for any decision being made. If you find there is more than one "D" in the mix, there may well be multiple decisions being made. Each decision should have a RAPID matrix and, if they are interdependent, ranking the decisions in decision order will provide clear expectations and timelines.

Having clarity how a decision is made significantly increases the effectiveness of any project or task. It also provides clear expectations for team members as to their role and responsivities relating to the decisions being made. Combined with the SMART Goals and Priority Matrix, teams and individuals will experience a higher level of effectiveness in both their influence of others' behaviors, and provide needed direction to achieve their desired results.

CHAPTER 5

Organizational LeadAbility

Levels of Leadership

Although we believe EVERYONE has the potential and developability to be A Better Leader, the reality of responsibility, accountability, and complexity is impacted by the scope of influence and experience of leaders at four distinct levels:

Everyday Leaders   Emerging Leaders   Established Leaders   Executive Leaders

- **Everyday Leaders** are individual contributors whose leadership development is primarily focused on self-leadership, expanding their influence and increasing their professional abilities.

- **Emerging Leaders** are individuals that have shown aptitude and a desire to expand their leadership to lead others, lead project teams, and explore leadership roles that provide influence beyond their individual role and function.

- **Established Leaders** are individuals that have solid experience in influencing beyond their role and function, often in positions leading departments, teams of teams, or cross-functional initiatives within the organization.

- **Executive Leaders** are individuals with organizational level responsibilities, influence requirements that go beyond the boundaries of the organization, often leading organizational units and enterprise-wide initiatives.

The Better Leadership Model is designed to create a common leadership language. Although everyone is a leader and can develop their LeadAbilities, we must recognize that the complexity and scope will be different depending on the employee's level of leadership.

As such, the application of each Leadership Choice and the LeadAbilities will be demonstrated differently depending on a person's leadership level. This differentiation is a key topic when having leadership development discussions to make sure that expectations are clearly set and outcomes are aligned with the level of leadership being discussed.

Leadership Development

Talent is an organization's most important resource. As such, an integrated talent management strategy is central to achieving an organizational mission and business results.

Leadership Development should focus on building the employee's current strengths and closing any gaps in relation to their current role –

and then for potential future roles. Numerous in-depth studies have reached the same conclusion: Organizations that invest in leadership development perform better than those that don't.

A recent report on leadership development put it this way:

> **"The message is clear – leadership development matters. It is hard to find a company which has survived many economic cycles that does not have a formal leadership development strategy in place. While it may take time to develop and refine, the results clearly pay off."**

We know there is a relationship between good people-management and employee commitment. Great leaders attract, hire, and inspire great people. Leadership development creates a magnet for high-performers and fosters a high-performance organization. This is why organizations that are 'built to last' have strong histories of leadership development.

The 70:20:10 Rule

Leadership development is NOT set of training courses to attend or a certification to achieve. It is a discipline and a continuous commitment to learning and growing.

The graphic below illustrates the 70:20:10 rule that describes how adults learn new behaviors and concepts.

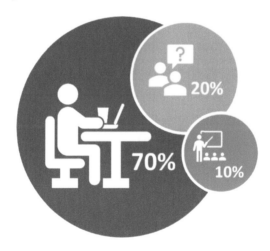

About 70% of organizational learning takes place on the job, through solving problems and through special assignments and other day-to-day activities.

Another 20% occurs through drawing on the knowledge of others in the workplace, from informal learning, from coaching and mentoring, and from support and direction from managers and colleagues.

Only 10% of learning and development occurs through more formal learning activities like classroom courses, workshops, or e-learning.

When creating a Leadership Development Plan, remember that development is not only about formal courses and programs or reading books and journals. People learn as much, if not more, through on-the-job development and training, shadowing others, opportunities to be a mentor for others, special projects, peer coaching, etc. Consider ALL sources of development support in helping a team member come up with their development plan.

A Five Step Process

Leadership development does not just happen. It takes a strong plan and purposeful actions on behalf of the people-manager and the employee being developed. As a people-manager, we recommend the simple Five Step Process for developing LeadAbility of employees you lead.

Discover Strengths and Development Areas

Establishing a RAPID Decision Matrix (see Chapter 4) for Leadership Development helps to set clear expectations with our employees. Having this decision matrix at the organizational level is also very helpful for people-managers to communicate timelines and budgetary constraints in developing leaders across the organization.

Assess the staff member's performance using the set of leadership behaviors and abilities in our Leadership Model to identify the employee's strengths and development areas. A strength is a behavior / ability that is demonstrated at or above the target level. A development area is a behavior / ability that is demonstrated below the target level.

At this time, you should also discuss development areas to ensure the employee remains engaged, challenged and their skills refreshed. Also consider the roles the employee aspires to and their competency strengths and development areas in relation to this role(s).

Determine the Development Priorities

In discussion with the employee, identify one or two leadership behaviors that are most important for the employee to focus on over the coming months. The primary focus of development should be on leadership behaviors, which the employee needs in their current role to meet and exceed expectations.

Once the employee is demonstrating the leadership behaviors at the required level, only then is it time to encourage them to start thinking about developing leadership behaviors which will be required in future roles. In identifying development areas, it is also important to be realistic about what is achievable by using the Priority Matrix (see Chapter 4). It may be more productive to focus on developing specific leadership behavior or ability than to try to develop a long list all at the same time.

Remember that someone may choose to develop a leadership behavior or ability to focus on even if it is a relative strength. If operating at a higher level will be important in a future role, then this is a reasonable area for development.

Design the Development Plan

After completing the previous steps, do not leave the design of the development plan to chance. Some managers like to create development plans for their employees, which is not recommended.

Instead, agree on the development goals for the year and identify specific objectives for each leadership behavior or ability that you have chosen to develop. Once you and the staff member have agreed on the leadership areas for the employee's development, help them to identify a specific development goal for each of them. In addition, help the employee to understand how developing a particular leadership behavior or ability links to and supports the successful achievement of their work goals and those related to the organizational goals and metrics.

It is important that the employee develops their own goals and that you do not come up with the goals for them. Encourage the employee to write their goals down in a SMART Goals format (see Chapter 4) and verbalize them clearly to you. By doing this, the employee is more likely to achieve the goal. Your role as the manager is to support and challenge, not to come up with the plan for them.

<u>Do and Debrief</u>

Once an employee's development plan has been agreed on, consider setting up regular (quarterly or monthly) meetings to catch up with the employee about their progress over the period. This will:

- Keep their goals the focus throughout the year for the employee and yourself.

- Provide an opportunity for you to help your employee with their workload so time can be best managed to incorporate development on-the-job.

- Give you an opportunity to provide feedback to the employee on your observations of any behavioral change following their development plan.

Remember that having a leadership development plan is not the goal – DOING the development and achieving the learning goals is the measurement of success!

Leadership Success Strategies

On both the Team and Organizational levels, it is important that we demonstrate our LeadAbilities in a way that best achieves the desired results. There are five Leadership Success Strategies that keep us focused on the needs of those we seek to influence and direct. As you can see by the graphic below, each Success Strategy aligns with a specific Skill Level we discussed in Chapter 4.

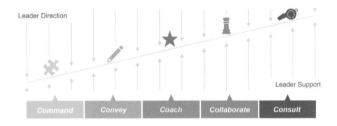

Leadership Success Strategies are built upon the belief that individuals and teams need different levels of Direction and Support based on their Skill Level. In the research we commonly refer to this dynamic as Situational Leadership, where a leader will adapt their behaviors to create the best opportunity for the individual or team to achieve their desired results.

Ken Blanchard and Paul Hersey were the pioneers of Situational Leadership and both the theory and the practice has evolved as more and more leaders learn to adapt their behaviors to meet the needs of others, rather than expect others to adapt to their styles of leadership, communication, decision-making, etc.

As mentioned earlier in this chapter, each Skill Level has two components – 1) the experience using the skill or ability, and 2) the consistency of excellence when demonstrating a skill or ability. Once we have determined the Skill Level, we align our behaviors with the matching Success Strategy.

Similar to Skill Level, each Success Strategy has two components – 1) the level of direction a leader provides, and 2) the level of support a leader provides. The levels of Direction and Support that are needed for an individual or team is determined by their Skill Levels.

Individuals and teams who have a lower Skill Level require a higher amount of Direction to be successful in achieving their desired results. As Skill Level grows, the amount of Direction is decreased. Individuals and teams who have a higher Skill Level require a higher level of Support and a diminishing level of Direction to be successful in achieving their desired results.

Command

This is the leadership strategy to demonstrate when supporting a *Novice*.

The leaders in this group support the **Novice** by making the decisions and informing the team member of decisions and tasks. The leader is actively involved and supervises the **Novice** closely. This is a top-down approach where the **Novice** executes what they are told to do. The **Novice** has almost no autonomy and are not pressured by decision making.

Convey

This is the leadership strategy to demonstrate when supporting an **Apprentice**.

The leaders in this group support the **Apprentice** by staying involved in day-to-day activities. The decisions ultimately lie with the leader, but input is required from the **Apprentice**. With this strategy the **Apprentice** is still supervised but has more autonomy and some decision-making influence.

Coach

This is the leadership strategy to demonstrate when supporting a **Specialist**.

The leaders in this group hand more responsibility to the **Specialist**. This leader still provides direction and decisions but reviews the facts with the *Specialist* before deciding. Leaders provide feedback to increase team members' confidence and motivation in a coaching manner. *Specialists* work closely with their leader to make decisions and accomplish the work.

<u>Collaborate</u>

This is the leadership strategy to demonstrate when supporting a *Master*.

Through sharing, the leaders in this group support the *Master* by defining boundaries of direction and execution, while the *Master* makes the decisions. This leadership style transfers ultimate responsibility to the *Master*, while monitoring the decision process. The *Master* is given a large amount of autonomy and has a high level of decision-making influence.

<u>Consult</u>

This is the leadership strategy to demonstrate when supporting a *Mentor*.

Through delegation, the leaders in this group support the Mentor with little involvement. The

Mentor is responsible for choosing the tasks and directions they will take. However, the leaders still stay involved for direction and/or feedback. The *Master* knows their role and performs with almost full autonomy and little supervision.

You may be asking, why is this in the Organizational Leadership chapter and not the Team Leadership chapter? That's a great question as the Success Strategies apply to both leading individuals as well as teams or groups. We chose to place the Success Strategies in the Organizational Chapter because it is often overlooked as a tool to use beyond the one-on-one leadership relationship. Based on the work of Hersey and Blanchard, Situational Leadership Theory is primarily taught in management courses as a strategy for one-on-one discussions. However, the theory also applies to groups and teams as a way to provide situational direction and support to maximize the desired team results.

For example, let's look at a Marketing Team that has an overall Skill Level of "Master" where they have advanced experience and consistently exceed the level of proficiency needed in their roles. In this situation, senior leaders need to demonstrate Collaboration, where expectations are established, and the Marketing Team is able to make collaborative decisions based on their extensive experience. However, if a new senior leader is appointed over the Marketing Team and they come in with a strong "Do As I Say" mindset with high Direction, not only the individual members, but the entire team can become disengaged.

If we look at a Call Center that has a constant influx of new team members, we could say the Call Center Team has an overall Skill Level of "Apprentice". They have some experience with varied level of consistency in the needed skills and abilities. In this situation, the senior leaders should be using a Convey Strategy, where decisions are made and then explained to the team. However, if a new senior leader is appointed over the Call Center and they come in with a Consulting approach, delegating authority and decision making to the team may not be the best choice given the Skill Level of that team.

Although the graphic shows defined boxes for each Leadership Strategy, it should be noted that they are more a continuum and have a flow rather than a step by step process. It should also be noted that determining Skill Level, and thus Success Strategy, is situational and requires a level of awareness, focus and energy from leaders. Being a "Situational Leader" is a choice to adapt our leadership behaviors in a way that will best equip, empower, enable, and encourage those that we lead.

CHAPTER 6

LeadAbility Styles and RelateAbility

Transformational Leadership

Transformational leaders hold positive expectations for followers, believing that each team member has the potential to contribute and develop. As a result, they equip, empower, enable, and encourage followers to exceed normal levels of performance.

Transformational leadership has been the focus of much research and organizational interest, as it aims to engage and motivate followers to rise above their own self-interest by altering their morale, ideals, interests, and values in order to motivate them to perform in a way that has the interests of the organization at heart.

Previous work looking at transpersonal leadership found that transformational leaders have the ability to transform an organization, largely as a result of their articulated motivational vision for the future. By clarifying and articulating a vision, they tend to motivate and empower their followers and organization employees to take responsibility to help to achieve that vision.

There are four LeadAbility Styles in A Better Leader Model and they are closely aligned with Transformational Leadership Theory.

Four LeadAbility Styles

A LeadAbility Style is a description of an individual's natural preference in how they influence and provide direction. In our Better Leader Model, we have four LeadAbility Styles based on theory and research in the field of

Transformational Leadership and TeamRelate Communication Styles.

Every individual has components of all four LeadAbility Styles and each Style has a natural alignment to the TeamRelate Communication Styles we presented in our book *RelateAbility*. Similarly, we each have a preferred LeadAbility Style and need to adapt our styles to maximize our Leadership effectiveness based on the employee skills, situation, or opportunity.

Empower

The Empower LeadAbility style is most closely aligned with the Director (D) Communication style. The primary goal and driving force of this style is to create purpose.

In Transformational Leadership theory, this is called "Inspirational Motivation." Someone who operates naturally from this style demonstrates the following Strengths, Interactions, and Mindsets:

Strengths

You need to lead, to manage, and to be in control. You tend to look to the future and plan for it. You set goals and have ideas about how to reach these goals. You tend to be curious about what could be. You have confidence that your ideas will work, and you can be open about the fact that you want those ideas to become the accepted way of doing things.

Interactions

You tend to be assertive, firm, and strong-willed, even forceful or demanding when necessary.

You prefer to keep things moving at a steady to fast pace. In any business matter, you like to get to the bottom line quickly. You may become annoyed with people who speak in generalizations or get onto tangents that are not directly related to the topic. You tend to be all business and rarely engage in frivolous banter.

Mindsets

You appreciate the approval of others as long as it is sincere. You respect people who are honest, trustworthy, and objective. You have little use for people who try to make good impressions with flattery or who are pretentious or overly impressed with themselves.

Your natural curiosity stays tuned to new, interesting challenges. If the conditions and timing are right, you like to become involved and make things happen. You like to be independent and free to think and act in ways that further your personal goals. You appreciate quality and want things done right. This style may also be reflected in orderliness and in being organized. You want others to take care of details and finish the project, but where things do not meet expected standards, you can become directly involved and hands-on.

You enjoy change, especially opportunities or activities that contribute to outcomes in which you have a vested interest. You tend to put more energy into organizing and initiating projects than in maintaining them once they are underway.

Encourage

The Encourage Leader style is most closely aligned with the Encourager (E) Communication Style. The primary goal and driving force of this style is to inspire greatness. In Transformational Leadership theory, this is called "Idealized Influence." Someone who operates naturally from this style demonstrates the following Strengths, Interactions, and Mindsets:

Strengths

You are a fast-paced, animated individual, who is very talkative and outgoing. You like to talk to just about anyone, anytime, anywhere. You tend to talk at a rapid rate and are quite fluent. You frequently use hand gestures to help get your points across. Your volume and variation in verbal expressions also may be distinguishing features.

You are jovial and fun-loving, and you try to keep it on the light side. You relate to people easily and have lots of friends.

Interaction

You are naturally enthusiastic, one who likes to encourage and motivate people. At these and other times, you need to be careful not to do all the talking, but to also listen and hear what people have to say. Listening is not a natural habit for you. You need to make a conscious effort to engage people in conversation so that it is not simply a monologue.

You are also diplomatic with an ability to say things that are socially acceptable and not abrasive or offensive. You dislike confrontations and avoid interpersonal conflict as much as possible.

Mindsets

You prefer to serve in a supportive role rather than being in charge. In the event a leadership role is required, you need to seek counsel from team members, superiors, or other respected authorities.

You can be very persuasive, and that translates into being a natural "seller." If the item is not an actual product, then you sell your opinions, ideas, or points of view. As an encourager, you have a soft-sell style and are seen as easy to relate to.

 Equip

The Equip Leader style is most closely aligned with the Facilitator (F) Communication Style. The primary goal and driving force of this style is to develop others. In Transformational Leadership theory, this is called "Individualized Consideration." Someone who operates naturally from this style demonstrates the following Strengths, Interactions, and Mindsets:

Strengths

You have a style that is warm, gentle, quiet, and reserved. You are friendly, respectful, and considerate of other people. You are naturally very patient, a trait that may be expressed by behaviors that are steady and dependable, planned and deliberate, not impulsive. You are serious-minded and are not generally inclined to joke around.

You are independent and able to get things done without being micro-managed or constantly told what to do. If the goal is clearly presented and understood, you tend to find ways to reach it, even if every detail about how to get there is not provided.

Interaction

People with this style tend to be thinkers as opposed to being highly talkative. You do not waste words, may be soft-spoken, and would rarely monopolize the conversation. However, when given the opportunity to facilitate, you are able to be a mediator and positively influence collaboration.

Mindsets

You prefer to work in environments that are calm and peaceful, where people get along with each other and there are few disturbances to the daily routine. You prefer plenty of time to complete assignments, invest in the skills and talents of others, and dislike deadlines or any task labeled "URGENT!" or "RUSH!"

You look to others for strong overall leadership and prefer to take a supportive role. However, you are also capable of solving problems independently and enjoy being trusted to do that, especially when they contribute directly to mentoring and coaching others.

 **Enable**

The Enable Leader style is most closely aligned with the Tracker (T) Communication Style. The primary goal and driving force of this style is to deliver excellence. In Transformational Leadership theory, this is called "Intellectual Stimulation." Someone who operates naturally from this style demonstrates the following Strengths, Mindsets, and Interactions.

Strengths

You are obsessed with doing things right. That means you rely on, and comply with, rules and regulations, policies and procedures, and respected authorities. For you, there is no substitute for excellence.

You like to take one step at a time. You probably keep a daily list of things to do and a schedule of events and activities and check them off when they are completed so that there is a sense of progress and clear evidence of accomplishment at the end of the day.

Interaction

You are more of a thinker than one who is outgoing and overly talkative. You choose words carefully so that few are wasted, and they are as accurate and direct and to the point as possible. You frequently back up statements with facts and figures or written documentation from respected authorities.

In areas of your expertise, standards are so high that the work of others typically fails to compare. Thus, your evaluations can often be constructively critical, including suggestions about how others should improve.

<u>Mindset</u>

You like, and use to great advantage, the latest systems and technologies because they provide valuable tools for managing information and maintaining order. You are conscientious, a person who follows up well, puts on the finishing touches, completes the task, and gets closure. You are extremely quality-oriented. While productivity is important, the quality of performance is more important. In fact, productivity undoubtedly is reduced because you put in so much time getting every detail done perfectly.

TeamRelate Communication Styles

The four TeamRelate Communication Styles are based upon the dimensions of focus and function

Communication Styles, and describe an individual's natural preference of focus and function. Every individual has components of all Communication Styles, but it is the strongest or most natural style that dominates the rest.

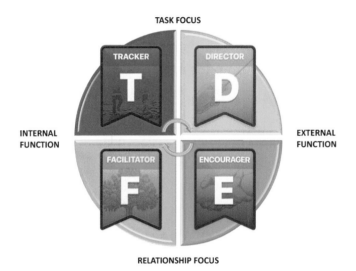

For quick reference, below is a summary of the four Communication Styles:

- **Director (D)**: The Director style refers to the degree to which an individual needs to be in charge or in control. They are highly task-focused and prefer to interact with and lead others.

- **Encourager (E):** The Encourager style refers to the degree to which someone is externally and socially oriented. They are highly relationship-focused and prefer to interact with and influence others.

- **Facilitator (F):** The Facilitator style refers to the degree to which an individual is purposeful and patient. They are highly relationship-focused and prefer to work in small groups or collaborate behind the scenes.

- **Tracker (T):** The Tracker style refers to the degree to which an individual is careful about "tracking down" and taking care of details. They are highly task-focused and prefer to work in small groups and lead processes.

The LeadAbility Styles are closely aligned with TeamRelate Communication Styles.

Connecting the Dots

A Leader Style is a description of an individual's natural preference in how they influence and provide direction. Every individual has components of all four LeadAbility Styles and each Style has a natural alignment to the TeamRelate Communication Styles. Similarly, we each have a preferred LeadAbility Style and need to adapt our styles to maximize our Leadership effectiveness based on the skill level of the employee and the situation or opportunity.

TeamRelate Communication			Transformational LeadAbility	
Style	Function	Focus	Style	Goal
Director	External	Task	**Empower**	To Create Purpose
Encourager	External	Relationship	**Encourage**	To Inspire Greatness
Facilitator	Internal	Relationship	**Equip**	To Develop Others
Tracker	Internal	Task	**Enable**	To Deliver Excellence

Similarly, the 12 LeadAbilities are demonstrated and deployed differently, based on the person's Communication Style and Transformational LeadAbility Style. However, we each have LeadAbilities that are more naturally aligned with the strengths and behaviors associated with our Communication Style and Leadership Style as shown on the next page.

Having a natural disposition to one of the LeadAbilities does not mean there is a level of expertise, just rather a more natural inclination to demonstrate and develop them. For example, we are born with our natural and preferred hand to write with, being right handed or left handed does not mean you are an effective writer or speller. These skills need to be developed to reach a level of mastery in each. Similarly, although it may be less comfortable to learn to write with your "other hand", it is possible to learn to do so with purposeful effort and practice.

TeamRelate Communication Style	Transformational LeadAbility Style	Naturally Aligned LeadAbilities
Director	Empower	• To Coach • To Deliver Results • To Think Strategically
Encourager	Encourage	• To Champion • To Communicate • To Include
Facilitator	Equip	• To Collaborate • To Develop • To Problem Solve
Tracker	Enable	• To Be Accountable • To Be Transparent • To Think Critically

CHAPTER 7

LeadAbility and Organizational Readiness

Organizational Readiness is a product of effective Organizational Leadership. We have talked about LeadAbility at the Organizational Level, the Levels of Leadership, and the importance of developing LeadAbilities at all levels of Leadership within our Organization.

In this chapter, we expand our Organizational Point of View beyond LeadAbility and into three critical components needed for Organizational Readiness:

- Maximizing Human Capital.
- Understanding Change.
- Creating a Learning Organization.

Maximizing Human Capital

Gallup research reports that 35% of workers report changing jobs in the last three years and slightly more than 50% of workers say they are actively seeking a new job or watching for job openings. On average, 50% of the employed workforce is considered "Not Engaged" in their employment. With only 30% of the employed workforce considered "Engaged", that leaves 20% of the employed workforce as "Actively Disengaged" and so unhappy in their workplaces that they actively undermine the success of the team and the organization.

Research among 1000 C-level executives worldwide identified the issues they were expecting to command their attention in the coming year. Of the 28 challenges from which they could choose, their biggest concerns were not issues relating to political instability, climate change, terrorism, or global recession. Instead, their top issues focused on their own leaders. "Developing Next Gen Leaders" and "Failure to Attract / Retain Top Talent" were rated in the top five by 65% of the executives. Research is clearly indicating that Human Capital, specifically leadership, is on the forefront of executive's priorities, and thus, a priority for the organizations they lead.

Furthermore, the results from the Global Leadership Forecast 2019 provide key insights for Human Capital Strategies. The research, sponsored by The Conference Board and DDI, is considered to be the most comprehensive leadership study of the last decade. Of the 2,500 global organizations surveyed:

- 35% of companies have high-potential development programs.

- 31% have a weak or non-existent relationship between annual strategic planning and their own plans to grow leadership talent.

- 65% do not believe their leaders have effective leadership development plans.

- 73% do not hold their leaders accountable for developing leaders on their teams.

- 52% do not know the up-to-date status of their leadership talent capability across the organization.

Additionally, in the six-year period between 2011 and 2017, the portion of organizations reporting sufficient leadership bench strength declined from an already low 42% to just above 38%. In the United States, that bench strength statistic is 14%, well below the global average.

What we are seeing is the foreshadowing of a Leadership Crisis as the older generations retire and companies lack the organizational readiness with talent that is ready to take the reins and continue the momentum of organizational growth and development.

The Human Capital Institute (HCI) is focused on innovations that help organizations get the maximum impact of their most valuable asset: people. They lead the market in research, application, and thought leadership in the area of maximizing human capital. Their model to understanding Talent Management and Human Capital is one of the best.

This model, which appears on the next page, has people as the core of organizational effectiveness.

Having a clearly understood Human Capital strategy that aligns with the business strategy is critical for an organization's success. Taking it a step further, making sure the Human Beings in the organization are in roles that maximize their effectiveness and are fully developed for taking on the next business need is a responsibility of those in Leadership Development.

When I have shared this graphic with clients, there is a moment of "ah-ha" in that the information is not necessarily new, but rather has been placed in the context that can help them create a more comprehensive human capital strategy. When an organization understands and actively makes decisions based on a strong human capital strategy, they create a state of readiness for those in the organization to effectively adapt to the ever-changing nature of our work world.

Truly innovative organizations reach beyond a need for "Human Doings" and embrace the vision of creating workplaces where every Human Being is empowered, encouraged, equipped, and enabled – bringing the best version of themselves to both their work and their lives.

In Leadership, it is critical for Human Capital Strategies to include the practices of identifying mission critical roles, resourcing talent based on performance and potential, and managing talent by assessing retention and risk of undesired turnover.

For each of these practices, it is imperative that the data be reviewed regularly, that a standard set of language and process be put in place to limit bias and unintended discrimination, and a commitment given to provide full transparency in the process and desired outcomes.

Identifying Potential and Performance

Having a strong bench strength for talent is critical to organizational readiness. Organizations need a standard process for reviewing the talent within the organization, often called Talent Review.

For some organizations, this is an annual process that is formal and integrates with the organizations' annual business planning. For other organizations, this is an ongoing process that integrates with quarterly or monthly talent discussions on performance, development, and career planning.

At the heart of any Talent Review is identifying talent that is high performing and high potential, resourcing that talent effectively, and making sure there is awareness of talent retention and talent risks.

Performance

Measuring performance in organizations is usually done on an annual basis. As part of a Talent Review process, it is important to identify the level of performance in "real time" and not assume that the performance measurement for the previous year is still relevant in the current organizational situation.

Performance should ALWAYS be based on CURRENT ROLE and not performance in previous roles. As our roles change, so does our responsibilities and ability to meet expectations in that new role. Maintaining a "NOW" mindset will help us better prepare for the "NEXT" when we move into Talent Planning based on the performance data.

For the purposes of Organizational Readiness, we use three levels to determine Performance rating. Many have been tempted to expand the rating scale to match their annual performance ratings (e.g. 1-5). However, this is not advised. The purpose of the Talent Review is to have current and real-time discussions on the talent bench strengths.

For the purposes of Organizational Readiness, Performance refers to WHAT the employee does and HOW they do it.

- **Low.** Weak performer. Inconsistently meets performance expectations. Often aligns with "(1) Unsatisfactory" or "(2) Needs Improvement" on annual performance reviews.

- **Medium**. Solid performer. Consistently meets and sometimes exceeds performance expectations. Often aligns with "(3) Meets Expectations" and "(4) Exceeds Expectations" on annual performance reviews.

- **High**. Strong performer. Consistently exceeds performance expectations and is sometimes referred to as the model of performance. Often aligns with "(5) Outstanding" on annual performance reviews.

Potential

Potential is one of the more difficult areas to rate as it is much more abstract and influenced by personal bias of leaders that are championing their team members. In an effort to help remove the personal bias and limit the influence of popularity, we have a three-level scale to evaluate potential:

- **Low**. Individual is capable of current role only. Individual could also be a bad fit for the role they are in.

- **Medium**. Individual is a good fit at current level and is capable of lateral move, or upward move only one level, in 12 - 18 months.

- **High**. Individual is a good fit in current role and is capable of either 1) immediate lateral or upward move one level and/or 2) upward mobility of more than one level in 12 - 18 months.

Potential includes raw ability, motivation to succeed, desire to move into a new or expanded role, and the commitment to the team or organization. We purposely limit our levels of potential to focus on readiness and capability of an individual to advance their role and responsibilities within a set timeframe.

For the purposes of Organizational Readiness, potential refers to the job level the individual is CAPABLE of attaining, provided continued performance and development.

We often get asked where "culture fit" comes into the discussion on performance and potential. As this term is often used as a shield for discriminatory practices, you will not see it within our process. However, the need to make sure that a person aligns effectively with the values and mission of an organization is still a real need.

Best practice should include both the **WHAT** and the **HOW** in evaluating people meeting their performance goals. I would not place someone as "High" in performance if they consistently exceed sales goals but do so in a way that creates hostility on the team, as this would not be living out the values of the organization. This assumes that the organization has a clearly defined set of values and a compelling purpose or mission statement.

Talent Planning 9-Box

McKinsey developed the 9 Box Matrix in the 1970s to help GE prioritize investments across its 150 business units. Not all business units were equally attractive. Some should receive investments and others should be divested. The 9 Box Matrix evaluated business units on two dimensions: industry attractiveness and competitive strength of the business unit.

Following the success of the 9Box for business planning, Human Resources teams co-opted this model as a talent management tool, and replaced the two industry axes with people specific ones: performance and potential. The main goal of the Talent Planning 9Box is to categorize employees, determine which to promote, retain and invest in, and which to reallocate.

The Talent Planning 9Box is an individual assessment tool that evaluates an employee's current and potential level of contribution to the organization. The horizontal rows of the grid indicate growth potential, and the vertical columns indicate current performance levels. The intersection of the two determines the employee's current standing and where development may be needed.

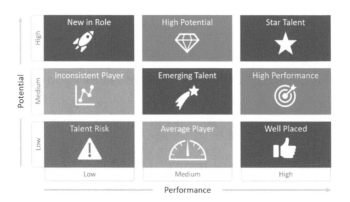

The above grid is most commonly used in talent planning as a method of evaluating an organization's current talent and identifying potential leaders. When leadership performance and potential are assessed and plotted on the graph, individuals in the upper right quadrant (often referred to as Box 1) are identified as candidates that are ready now for advancement, while those in the lower left quadrant (often referred to as Box 9) may need to be reassigned or removed from the organization.

The boxes on the grid indicate where investment needs to be made to develop future leaders. Those people identified as Star Talent should be ready for top leadership within six months to a year; those identified as High Potential and High Performance have a longer timeline but can be further developed to reach the level of Star Talent.

Star Talent

The individuals in this box are rated as High Performance and High Potential. They consistently perform well in a variety of assignments and each is a big picture thinker, problem solver, and self-motivated. They may be seen as a key influencer across multiple business units / functions within the organization. Recommended actions include:

- Stretching for larger role, focused development for future role.
- Stretching goals / cross functional assignments and leadership rotations.
- Creating development plan targeting leadership disciplines and other skills relevant to next move.

Star Talent should be assigned an executive mentor within the organization. If they truly are High Performing and High Potential, they should have an increased executive presence and further build relationships at the higher levels of the organization.

High Potential

The individuals in this box are rated High Potential and Medium Performance. They do well at their current roles meeting all targets with capacity/ability to do more. A focus on improving consistency of performance is the key focus with these individuals. Recommended actions include:

- Coaching to enhance performance.

- Looking for opportunities for growth and new experiences to demonstrate proficiency and performance.

- Giving stretch assignments within the scope of the current role to help prepare for next level of performance expectations.

High Potential talent are often referred to as "Diamonds in the Rough" as they have the potential to take on more responsibility, but need experiences that can challenge their performance to consistently exceed in their current role.

High Performance

The individuals in this box are rated High Performance and Medium Potential. They often exceed targets/goals but have development gaps within their current role. The focus for High Performers is furthering their knowledge, skill, and experiences to provide a better understanding of the organization, beyond their own role. Recommended actions include:

- Looking for opportunities to expand role with cross-functional impact.
- Challenging to focus on strategic/big picture thinking.
- Creating a Leadership Development Plan to enhance leadership skills.

High Performance talent are often referred to as "Subject Matter Experts" in that they have a mastery level of the skills needed in their current role. Often, they are targeted for promotion, when they are not yet in a place to effectively lead or manage cross-functional projects or initiatives. Giving them experiences to grow in this area will often cause them to self-select out of promotions if advancing into formal leadership is not part of their career plan.

The remaining boxes can be used to identify when coaching or a change in job or responsibilities may be needed. During a formal Talent Review discussion, the remaining boxes are often not discussed due to the volume of individuals and the time needed to purposefully discuss each box.

Additionally, ongoing performance and development discussions should be happening on a regular basis between team members and their managers. Research has shown that engagement and performance increase when there is ongoing communication between managers and their direct reports, providing clear expectations, regular feedback on performance, and purposeful development discussions.

<u>New in Role</u>

The individuals in this box are rated High Potential and Low Performance. This rating is usually due to the individual being new to their role. They have High Potential rating as there is a belief that they are fully qualified for their role, but have not had time enough in that role to fully demonstrate performance. Recommended actions include:

- Ensuring effective onboarding and team integration.

- Setting clear expectations for role and providing regular feedback.

- Making sure their manager is receiving coaching to maximize effectiveness.

If Talent Reviews are being completed annually, it would be unusual for an individual to appear in this box year after year. If an individual is appearing year after year in the New to Role box, they are being improperly rated. However, it is common to have an individual move from the Star Talent box to the New in Role as they promote into a new role because of Talent Planning.

<u>Emerging Talent</u>

The individuals in this box rate as Medium Performance and Medium Potential. They consistently meet targets/goals, have stable potential, and strong performance. Recommended Actions include:

- Coaching to enhance performance and develop skills.

- Allowing opportunities for growth and new experiences.

- Providing opportunities for mentoring and subject matter expertise.

They are also known as "Core Performers" and can be expected to place in this box every year. Ongoing conversations with the individual may show a desire for advancement and managers may consider job enlargement at their same level, provided the manager can make the coaching commitment required to do so.

Well Placed

The individuals in this box rate as High Performance and Low Potential. They are experienced high performers but may have reached their limit in current career path. They are often seen as Subject Matter Experts. Recommended actions include:

- Leveraging subject matter expertise on process improvement projects within their area of expertise.

- Providing opportunities to champion culture and change initiatives that align with their current role.

- Rewarding and recognizing their value to the team and organization.

Some management philosophies dismiss the value of these Well-Placed individuals. This is a mistake. These individuals are often the champions of the organization's culture and values, providing a reinforcing energy and setting the standard for others within the organization.

Average Player

The individuals in this box rate as Medium Performance and Low Potential. They are effective performers in their role, but may also have reached their career potential. Recommended actions are:

- Providing incentive to reach higher levels of performance in their current role.

- Providing lateral development opportunities to increase organizational knowledge.

- Rewarding and recognizing their value to the team and organization.

Average Players are usually interested in opportunities to expand their roles but have not yet reached high performance in the role they have. Lateral development assignments, where they can be exposed to areas of the organization and meeting with their peers may have a positive impact on their performance.

Best practice is to have a second review session to discuss and determine an action plan for those that are a Talent Risk and Inconsistent Players. It is a leadership failure to have the same person in these two boxes for consecutive review sessions. Prior to a second Talent Review, individuals in these boxes should have either been successful in increasing their performance to meet expectations, or they should have been moved to another role that better fits their skill sets (either in the organization or outside the organization).

Inconsistent Player

The individuals in this box are weak and inconsistent with their performance. They may talk of a desire to advance and grow, but their performance does not align with their desire.

These individuals often require a high level of management and oversight as their inconsistent performance negatively impacts others on the team or may cause challenges with projects and change initiatives. Recommended actions include:

- Establishing clear expectations in a Performance Improvement Plan.

- Reducing job assignments to bring performance up in core responsibilities.

- Reviewing performance within 90 days of Talent Review.

This box is often referred to as "Manage Up or Manage Out" as there is some level of potential that is not being demonstrated, or possibly they have been incorrectly resourced (their talent is better placed elsewhere in the organization). If they are incorrectly resourced, they must present a consistent level of performance in their current role before being "handed off" to another manager.

Talent Risk

The individuals in this box pose a credible threat to the well-being of their team and to the organization. Individuals with Low Performance and Low Potential can also be Actively Disengaged, compounding the negative impact of their performance. Recommended actions include:

- Initiating immediate determination of future employment status.

- Creating a Performance Improvement Plan (if warranted).

- Providing a dignified exit from the organization.

Individuals that present themselves as a Talent Risk in one organization, may become Star Talent in another organization. Regardless of action, an individual should NEVER be in this box consecutively. Having an individual remain a Talent Risk and not quickly improving performance is a leadership failure. An evaluation should also be made on any possible differentials in the presented job description and the realities expected in the role.

When used correctly, the Talent Planning 9Box can be both a versatile and a valuable tool to include as part of a Human Capital Strategy. However, as with any tool, it must be used with a level of integrity and consistency, thereby requiring a level of oversight and purposeful management.

Assessing Talent Retention Risk

Retention of talent is a critical measure of success in any organization. While not all loss is bad, unplanned loss has significant impact on morale, engagement, and productivity. Having a tool to help identify Retention Risk is helpful, especially as part of a larger Talent Management / Leadership Development Plan.

The tool we use to help visualize the data regarding retention is called a "Retention Risk Matrix". One axis is the Probability of Leaving and the other is Impact of Loss.

Probability of Leaving / Flight Risk

This data set refers to the PERSON that is being discussed. The focus is on understanding how likely the person is to leave the organization and the timeframe for that probability. Many factors play into an employee's Flight Risk although most notable is attendance, performance, and attitude in their current role. For assessing Probability of Leaving / Flight Risk, we use the following three levels:

- **Low**. Anticipate employee will not choose to leave the organization in the next 12 months.

- **Medium**. Anticipate the employee could choose to leave the organization in 6-12 months.

- **High**. Anticipate the employee will choose to leave the organization in 0-6 months.

Impact of Loss / Business Risk

This data set refers to the POSITION that is being discussed. The focus is on understanding how readily available replacement talent is for the position. Also being considered is the impact to operational effectiveness and business performance. Retention is often looked at from only the business operations and the impact of having no one in the role that is being reviewed. It is important to also include the availability of talent with skills needed for that role, as the smaller the available talent pool, the longer it will take to fill the role, further impacting business performance. For assessing Impact of Loss / Business Risk, we use the following three levels:

- **Low**. Replacement talent is readily available. Impact to business operations is average.

- **Medium**. Replacement talent is available with moderate effort and sourcing. Impact to business operations is significant.

- **High**. Replacement talent is difficult or costly to acquire. Impact to business operations is severe.

Understanding the Matrix

Using the data gathered for the PERSON and the POSITION, place the Name of the Person in the appropriate box on the Retention Risk Matrix.

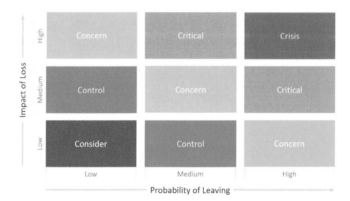

Based on their placement, names will appear in one of five Retention / Risk categories:

- **Crisis**. Individuals in this box have both a High Probability of Leaving and a High Impact of Loss. This requires immediate attention to determine if there is an option for a Retention Plan or if there is "Ready Now" successors for the role. If this person appears in the Talent Planning 9Box as a High Potential, High Performer, or Talent Star, the impact will be increased as the loss would not only remove the person from the role, but also remove them from any plans to have them fill roles that are anticipating a need for succession.

- **Critical**. Individuals in these boxes have a High rating for either Probability of Leaving or Impact of Loss with a Medium rating of the other variable. Although not a Crisis, the unplanned vacancy of this position will incur significant to severe impact on the business, either in operations, or in the acquiring of talent to fill the open role. Further complicating the Retention Risk will be the person's location on the Talent Planning 9Box.

- **Concern.** Individuals in these boxes should be reviewed more regularly as to any changes in their Probability of Leaving rating. A Flight Risk evaluation could be conducted to determine the reasons that impact the Probability of Leaving.

- **Control.** Individuals in these boxes require a level of management control to be initiated. If the individuals listed rate Medium Business Impact and Low Probability of Leaving, an evaluation of the succession for the role is advised. If the individuals listed rate Medium Probability of Leaving but Low Business Impact, they may be misplaced in their role and career planning is advised.

- **Consider**. The final box refers to those whose overall Retention Risk is not cause for Concern, Critical Review, or immediate Crisis Action. The individuals in these boxes do not require any specific action at this time.

It is not feasible to conduct a Retention Risk analysis on every role in the organization, or for every person. As such, it is advised that leaders identify Mission Critical Roles that, due to their impact to the organization's mission and well-being should be reviewed for Retention Risk on a regular basis. As business change is becoming the norm for many organizations, it is recommended to review which roles are Mission Critical as part of a formal Talent Review process.

Understanding Change

There have been decades of research on how people experience change at the individual level, the group level, and at the organizational level. The Change Curve has become the empirical standard that we use to gain more awareness of how change impacts people, what they experience and what they need to successfully move from a mindset of "just survive" to one where "we thrive". There are six stages to The Change Curve. Below is just an overview of each stage. We dig deeper into understanding change in our book *AdaptAbility*.

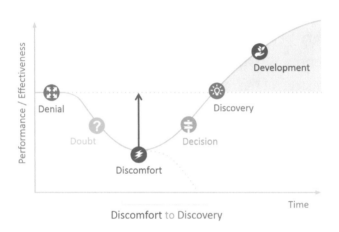

Discomfort to Discovery

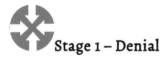

Stage 1 – Denial

Stage 1 often starts with shock and a sense of loss – whether or not the change is "good" like a job promotion or welcoming a new baby to the family, or "bad" like getting laid off or having a family member pass away. Our first reaction will be one of denial. We can't believe this situation is happening and our minds race to find some sense of stability and sanity. Being in Stage 1 feels almost like driving in the fog, unable to clearly see the road ahead yet, for your own safety, you must keep moving forward. Feeling almost nothing, we go on "auto-pilot" while trying to make sense of what we just heard or experienced. At this stage, our primary focus in on self-protection and a need to create a sense of personal safety and stability.

Stage 2 – Doubt

Stage 2 brings our mind into the situation. We begin to assemble our thoughts about our circumstances and seek to gather more information. Doubt also triggers emotions like anger and frustration, causing resentment and blame to be our go-to behaviors. When new information is presented, we will doubt the facts given and even doubt our own doubts. If we aren't careful we can get stuck in an "us vs. them" pattern of thinking that creates a wall for any new and often important information, to be heard and understood. At this stage, our primary focus is on being "right" and a need to gather facts and information to help process the shift we are experiencing.

 Stage 3 – Discomfort

Stage 3 creates a wave of emotional response. Anxiety, confusion, and feelings of being overwhelmed are common to this stage. This often progresses into a sense of depression or longing for how things used to be. During this stage, there is a natural tendency to experience a lag or decrease in our performance and effectiveness.

In this stage we may think that we are "off our game" or that we "really just don't care anymore" when asked about the change or shift we are experiencing. At this stage, our primary focus is on the problem to solve, and a need to reframe our perspective considering the larger view of the situation or circumstance.

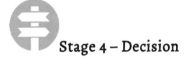

Stage 4 – Decision

Stage 4 is all about making decisions and taking action. The first three stages had us "stuck in the past". Now we turn our face towards the sun and the bright future that this shift will bring with it. It is in this stage that we need to choose to take action, any action, that will move us forward.

Leveraging creativity, seeking ways to do things better, and embracing the opportunity to be an active participant in the change – these are the hallmark characteristics of this stage. It is in this stage that we welcome opposing views, we search for viable options, and have a renewed decisiveness. At this stage our primary focus is on finding solutions and a need to contribute to the path moving forward.

Stage 5 – Discovery

Stage 5 is all about discovery and determination. We begin to grasp the meaning of the shift and enjoy a deeper understanding of the benefits and potential of this new way of being. We are energized, hopeful, and yet realize we haven't reached the finish line yet. In this stage we are challenged to finish strong and achieve what we have already determined to be our success in the situation or circumstance we find ourselves.

At this stage we are able to begin to realize the important insights and learning that have occurred in the process of our shift. We are in a heightened learning mode, seeking to build upon what we have learned about ourselves, about others, and about the very nature of change itself. At this stage our primary focus is on achievement and a need to fully integrate the insights we have gained.

 Stage 6 – Development

Stage 6 is all about development and giving back. As the shift seems to become a memory and what was "new" now has become our "normal". We have reached the end of The Change Curve, yet feel there is still more we can do with what we have experienced. Here we realize we have fully transitioned from a survival mode to actually thriving beyond the situation or shift that began our journey through change.

When we can experience positive changes that result in our reaching this stage, we build resilience and adaptability for ourselves. and, we realize that our experience has equipped us to help others as they transition through the same or similar shifts in their personal or work lives. We find the joy of being an advocate, support, mentor, or coach to others, allowing our insight and learning to be shared and leveraged in another person's change journey. At this stage our primary focus is on continuous improvement and a need to reach out to better others that need our help and support.

Remember that these stages of change occur at each Point of View – the individual, the group / team, and the organization / community. Building a Culture of LeadAbility requires a planned and purposeful approach to managing the change from the current state of your organization to the future state of an organization that has leaders equipped, empowered, encouraged, and engaged at every level.

Becoming a Learning Organization

When Gallup asked people across generations why they left their last job, the most common words used were "growth," "opportunity," and "development." Research also showed that 91% of US workers say the last time they expanded their skill and ability, they had to leave their company to do so at another organization.

Building a Culture of LeadAbility means that there is continuous improvement of the processes, practices, and people. David Garvin of Harvard University addresses this question in his research. He contends that continuous improvement requires a commitment to organizational learning. Organizations that have this commitment to ongoing learning as part of their culture are called "Learning Organizations".

Research shows that Learning Organizations are healthier places to work because they:

- Encourage independent thought and reasoning.
- Increase ability to manage change.
- Improve processes and quality outcomes.

- Provide positive morale and a vision of the future.
- Develop a more engaged workforce.
- Stretch and strengthen perceived limits.
- Connect with personal need to belong, learn, and grow.

Let's look at four components needed to support a company's mission to become a Learning Organization.

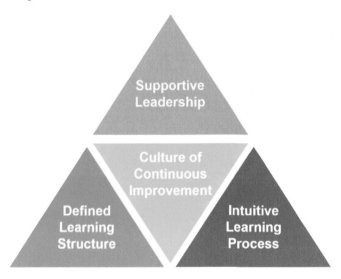

Supportive Leadership

The top of the pyramid is the most visible and here we find our first component of a Learning Organization: Supportive Leadership.

It is important that top leaders have clear vision and goals related to being a Learning Organization. Additionally, they must make sure the beliefs and values of the organization are aligned from top to bottom and between functions and departments. Critical leadership components are Credibility and Managerial Trust. Building credibility and trust, at is simplest form, is Doing What You Said You Would Do (or DWYSYWD for short). To champion change by word only is just public relations and "fluff". It takes leaders that are willing to roll up their sleeves and be actively engaged in the change, and proactively seek out those that demonstrate the commitment to continuous learning. If these are missing within the organization, the leadership won't have the influence and power necessary to build a culture of continuous improvement.

Once there is clarity in vision and mission, alignment of culture with the goals of continuous change, and leadership that has built credibility and trust – it is now necessary to have practices and policies in place that will reinforce the desired behaviors. Remember, when creating these reinforcing processes, that people want to be engaged and equipped, not cattle prodded and criticized. Knowing the behaviors desired and placing positive reinforcement when achieved, is the surest way to building engagement around a continuous learning culture.

Similar to needing to align the walk with the talk, supporting leaders need to make a commitment to being measured on the results. If there is "no money where the mouth is", the initiative to make culture of continuous learning will eventually fall by the wayside. People move when they are being measured. Leadership prioritizes performance metrics, especially when the metrics are linked to pay.

Overall, to create a Learning Organization and a culture of continuous improvement, there must be voice and action at the top of the organization to support it.

Culture of Continuous Improvement

One of the primary forces in building a culture of continuous improvement is Psychological Safety. This is a term that I wish more organizations and leaders were actively aware of.

In short, experimenting or learning new things naturally causes anxiety. To have a culture where employees are encouraged to experiment and stretch themselves in their development, it is important to reinforce that there is Psychological Safety. Psychological Safety means that the pain and discomfort of unlearning or relearning will be possible, worthwhile, and supported.

In addition to Psychological Safety, a culture of continuous improvement requires the following four characteristics: Appreciation of Differences, Openness to New Ideas, Allocation of Time and Resources to Learning, and Communication of Progress. The story of the Sticky Note by 3M is a great example of how these factors enabled an initial experiment to become the largest revenue generating product for the organization.

Defined Learning Structure

To support the continuous learning culture, there needs to be a defined learning structure in place to support it. A Learning Organization will make sure to have formal processes, tools, and training to equip and empower new learning and improvement.

As such, there will need to be, at a minimum, a path for Experimentation, a process for Information Collection, a means to Analyze the Information, and a method of Measurement to determine if progress has been made. Additionally, there will need to exist a protocol for Information Transfer where experimenters and learners can share their knowledge, encourage each other, and hopefully spark insight and innovation.

Intuitive Knowledge Workers

Instituting training and tools in a defined structure is significantly easier than attaining and retaining intuitive knowledge workers in an organization. We tend to forget that everything we have NOW was once a WOW! in someone's mind. The amazing technology we hold in our hands, the ability to travel around the globe in hours instead of weeks, the medical tools to determine our ancestry by DNA, and the incredible knowledge base of the Internet – these all were created by people who were committed to new ideas and continuous improvement. So, what do these great minds have in common? They share a commitment to the following five concepts:

1. **Systems Thinking** is the ability to view life as a pattern of happenings versus isolated events. Individuals with high systems thinking see how events and decisions interact and interconnect. They understand that one act, like stubbing your toe, will have repercussions on the functioning of the system, not just the toe.

2. **Personal Mastery** focuses on being committed to the best an individual can be within their natural capabilities. Individuals with high personal mastery love learning and strive to be the best person they can be. They are realistic in what they can accomplish while committed to reaching their full potential.

3. **Mindfulness** is all about mental models. Each person looks at life differently, based on their experiences, education, and effects of decisions made by themselves and others on their well-being. Individuals with high mindfulness realize that their mental models may not perfectly reflect realty. While they will have specific points of view, they are open to hear others. A level of self-awareness and self-reflection are required to increase mindfulness.

4. **Shared Visions** requires having a vision and a willingness to share that vision with others. Envisioning the future opportunities, seeing potential, and being able to articulate that vision is only half of the Shared Visions battle. To be successful, an individual must also have the confidence and competence to effectively communicate that vision in a way that will connect with others and become shared. As such, building employee RelateAbility provides the foundation to more effectively build and maintain relationships by understanding Communication Styles and Core Convictions of those we work with.

5. **Team Learning** does not occur because you have called a group of people a "team". Often, we substitute the title for the discipline needed to foster a culture of continuous improvement. Team learning is about the process of developing TeamAbility – being interdependent, contributing to a shared vision / goal, working together to attain it, and the ability to create new learning from each team experience. True team learning creates high levels of trust and accountability within the

team and contributes to a culture of continuous improvement.

The above concepts were originally resulted from Dr. Senge's research in 1990 on Learning Organizations. As we dig deeper into understanding organizational culture, we realize that the individual employees are the "heart" of any culture initiative, including creating a Learning Organization and culture of continuous improvement. As such, what we seek in the culture, we must also seek in the individuals that we employ.

Building a culture of continuous improvement and/or becoming a Learning Organization is not a "Quarterly Initiative" that has chosen start and completion dates. Making this choice is an act of Culture Change and one that will take years to fully integrate into an organization. Calling yourself a "Learning Organization" as part of marketing may benefit in the short term. But customers and employees that are truly aligned with the principles of continuous learning and innovation will become frustrated and, quite simply, leave.

Your employees will notice if your organization is not actively discussing Organizational Culture at the top and making purposeful decisions that support your stated vision, mission, and values. And they will respond accordingly.

CHAPTER 8

Improving Your LeadAbility

We have come to the end of the book. A lot of ground has been covered in a short amount of time. Our hope is that you are wanting to improve your LeadAbility. With all this learning, we now have the Choice to be better, or set this book down and move onto another. As we reflect on all the information we have covered, there are four recommended actions that, if consistently practiced with purpose, will further deepen and improve our LeadAbility.

Live Wholeheartedly

Brene Brown is a Sociologist, researcher, professor and amazing author whose research has explored topics related to trust, leadership, vulnerability, and how critical connection and belonging are to our well-being. Brene's TED talk on the Power of Vulnerability transformed the way I communicate, consult, teach, parent, and ultimately lead in both my personal and professional life.

A key area of her research has been identifying ways we can bring our whole selves to our work and relationships. She calls this Wholehearted Living and has identified 14 Guideposts that we can use to help us identify the things we need to cultivate in our lives and those things that we need to purposefully let go of to maximize our potential in our work and lives. They are:

- Cultivate Authenticity → Letting Go of What Other People Think

- Cultivate Self-Compassion → Letting Go of Expecting Perfectionism

- Cultivate a Resilient Spirit → Letting Go of Numbing and Powerlessness
- Cultivate Gratitude and Joy → Letting Go of Scarcity and Fear
- Cultivate Intuition and Trust → Letting Go of the Need for Certainty
- Cultivate Creativity → Letting Go of Comparison with Others
- Cultivate Play and Rest → Letting Go of Productivity as Self-Worth
- Cultivate Calm and Stillness → Letting Go of Anxiety as a Lifestyle
- Cultivate Meaningful Work → Letting Go of Self-Doubt and Supposed-To
- Cultivate Laughter and Flow → Letting Go of Always Being in Control

As you can see, each Guidepost is like a coin. On one side is the practices we can Cultivate. Cultivating is about creating space for growth, moving forward and developing new skills, abilities, and experiences. On the other side is the practice of Letting Go. To let go is to remove obstacles and detach from skills, abilities, and experiences that may be holding us back. To maximize our Wholehearted Living, we must do both. We must create the space for growth and also release the things that limit us from reaching our full potential.

On a final note, Dr. Brown was specific in her choice of the word Guideposts as living wholeheartedly is not a destination to be reached, rather a journey we pursue.

"Wholeheartedness is like a North Star. You can never get there. But you know when you are heading in the right direction."

Dr. Brene Brown

As you seek to improve your LeadAbility, these Guideposts help us to keep grounded in our development. They require us to apply our will and heart to be the best versions of ourselves in both our work and our life outside of the workplace.

Learn Continuously

In our discussion of Leadership, we have talked about choosing to Listen to Learn, further our development through learning and experience, and the components of a Learning Organization. Learning is such a critical component of growing and developing, both personally and professionally.

I have used the LEARN acronym to help remind me of what it means to Learn Continuously – seeking opportunities to grow and develop my own skills and to expand my understanding of others, their cultures, beliefs, and practices. Ultimately, learning for the purposes of bettering myself and those I serve.

- LISTEN. To listen is to take the time to actually listen, not just hear what is being said. Here we seek to understand the point of view others are sharing before trying to share my own point of view that I want them to understand. Active listening means making sure that we actually understand what others are saying by repeating what they said and making sure they feel heard and can provide clarity on areas where we may have misunderstood.

- **EXPLAIN.** After seeking to understand first, then I have the opportunity to share my views, beliefs, or perceptions of the situation or problem; sharing in a way where others will feel a valued part of the conversation and in a way that seeks genuine connection and contribution. Here I allow others to actively listen and repeat what I have said to make sure they understood my explanation, allowing me to create clarity and respond calmly to make sure mutual understanding is achieved.

- **ACKNOWLEDGE.** Now we have a clear understanding of each other's perspective. A critical step in continuously learning is to acknowledge that there are both similarities and differences in the way others understand a situation and the way I understand it to be. We are not yet seeking agreement, rather acknowledging the specific areas where we have similarities and where we have differences. We will not agree with everyone and we cannot expect others to always agree with us.

- **R**ECOMMEND. Here we start the process of ideation, or the generating of ideas in an attempt to create a win-win solution. We are open to all ideas that will help in all parties achieving their desired results. Compromise may be required, and doing so with compassion and understanding is critical to planning a course of action.

- **N**AVIGATE. Some LEARN models use the word "Negotiate" and that seems too adversarial. Learning continuously is all about navigating each situation to create a solution, moving from an obstacle mentality to an opportunity mindset, moving forward to a future that is built upon dignity, compassion, integrity, and respect.

What an incredible world and workplace we would have if we, as leaders, chose to Learn Continuously – taking every moment in our lives, be they good or bad, and seeking ways to grow and develop from them. Then furthering our leadership legacy by mentoring and coaching others to learn continuously to achieve their potential in both their life and work.

Lead Courageously

One of my favorite sayings is "Education without Application is just Useless Information!" Having Awareness without it impacting Behavior, runs the same result – a good read, but no real change. Taking the LEAD isn't about taking control or power in a shifting situation or circumstance. Taking the LEAD reflects the following:

- LEARN. As mentioned already, challenge yourself to be a life-long learner. Immerse yourself in new ideas and insights, especially those that are different than your own. For me, I absolutely love listening to TedTalks on TED.com, sometimes I just randomly select one to learn something new or gain a new insight on how others see our world.

- ENGAGE. Challenge yourself to connect with others and participate in leadership initiatives. We are all hard wired for connection. Understanding ourselves is powerful, but connecting and engaging in great conversation and learning about others brings a whole new level to living your best life. Proactively seeking ways to make a difference, no matter how small, is still choosing to engage in the life you are living.

- **A**PPRECIATE. Challenge yourself to seek opportunities to communicate your appreciation to others for their behaviors and choices. There is a proverb that says, "What You Seek, You Will Find". Choose to seek the good in others, the beauty in a moment, the benefit of the change, or simply be grateful for the breath you breathe.

- **D**ELIVER. Challenge yourself to be accountable, to do what you say you will do. So many great ideas and efforts fail because we don't deliver on what we have promised. I love the saying by Dr. Arnold Beckman: "There is no substitute for excellence." Make it a habit to under promise and over deliver as we seek excellence in all we choose to do.

and, Choose Better

To close out the book, I want to share a pledge that I have used to challenge myself and my LeadAbility. I have used the following pledge with students, employees, clients, peers, friends, and family to help anchor our will and our choice to be better.

A Better Leader Pledge
I will be better today
than I was yesterday.
I will be better tomorrow
than I am today.

Every day I will choose to
Live Wholeheartedly,
Learn Continuously, and
Lead Courageously.

As a result,
I will better my own life,
the lives of those around me,
and the world we live in.

My hope is that this book has challenged you to see yourself as a leader, to recognize the opportunities to further develop your LeadAbility, and to positively influence others' behavior and provide needed direction to achieve your desired results.

Research and Resources

Adair, J.E. (1988). Effective leadership. London. Pan Books.

Adair, J.E. (1973). "Action-centered leadership". McGraw-Hill, London.

Alimo-Metcalfe, B.; Alban-Metcalfe, J. (2005). Leadership: time for a new direction? Leadership, 1 (1), 51-71.

Antonakis, J.; Avolio, B. J.; Sivasubramaniam, N. (2003). "Context and leadership: An examination of the nine-factor Full-Range Leadership Theory using the Multifactor Leadership Questionnaire". The Leadership Quarterly. 14 (3): 261–295. doi:10.1016/S1048-9843(03)00030-4.

Avery, G. C. (2005). Understanding leadership. London: Sage Publications.

Balwant, Paul T. (2016-02-01). "Transformational Instructor-Leadership in higher education teaching: a meta-analytic review and research agenda". Journal of Leadership Studies. 9 (4): 20–42. doi:10.1002/jls.21423.

Balwant, Paul T. (2019). "Stay close! The role of leader distance in the relationship between transformational leadership, work engagement, and performance in undergraduate project teams". Journal of Education for Business. 21 (4): 376–393. doi:10.1177/1548051813502086.

Barling, J., & Cooper, C. L. (2008). The SAGE Handbook of Organizational Behavior. Vol. 1: Micro Approaches. Thousand Oaks, CA: SAGE.

Bass, Bernard M. (1985). Leadership and performance beyond expectations. New York: Free Press.

Bass, Bernard M. (1990). "From transactional to transformational leadership: Learning to share the vision". Organizational Dynamics. 18 (3): 19–31. doi:10.1016/0090-2616(90)90061-S.

Bass, Bernard M. (1999). "Two decades of research and development in transformational leadership" (PDF). European Journal of Work and Organizational Psychology. 8: 9–32. doi:10.1080/135943299398410.

Bass, Bernard M. (2014). Transformational leadership (3rd ed.). New York, NY: Routledge.

Bass, Bernard M (2006). Transformational leadership. Riggio, Ronald E. (2nd ed.). Mahwah, N.J.: L. Erlbaum Associates. ISBN 978-0805847611. OCLC 59360173.

Barth-Farkas, Faye; Vera, Antonio (2014). "Power and transformational leadership in public organizations". International Journal of Leadership in Public Services. 10(4): 217–232. doi:10.1108/ijlps-07-2014-0011.

Bennis, W. (1994). On becoming a leader. (Rev. ed). Reading, MA: Perseus Books.

Bernard M. (2000). "The future of leadership in learning organizations". Journal of Leadership Studies. 7 (3): 18–40. doi:10.1177/107179190000700302.

Blake, R.R., Mouton, J.S. (1985). The managerial grid III: the key to leadership excellence. Houston: Gulf Publishing Co.

Blanchard, K.H., Zigarmi, P., Zigarmi, D. (1985). Leadership and the one minute manager: increasing effectiveness through situational leadership. New York: Morrow.

Bligh, Michelle C., and James R. Meindl. "2 The cultural ecology of leadership: an analysis of popular leadership books." The Psychology of Leadership: New Perspectives and Research. Ed. David M. Messick andRoderick M. Kramer. Mahwah, NJ: Lawrence Erlbaum Associates, 2005. 11-36.

Bolman, L., Deal, T. (1991). Reframing organizations. San Francisco: Jossey-Bass.

Brewer C.S., Kovner C.T., Djukic M., Fatehi F., Greene W., Chacko T.P. & Yang Y. (2016). "Impact of transformational leadership on nurse work outcomes". Journal of Advanced Nursing. 72 (11): 2879–2893. doi:10.1111/jan.13055. PMID 27346330.

Bryman, A. (1996). Leadership in organizations. In Clegg S. R., Hardy, C. and Nord, W. R. (Eds). Handbook of Organization Studies, pp.276-292. London: Sage.

Burns, J.M. (1978). Leadership, New Your, Harper and Row.

Burns, J.M. (2004). Transformational leadership. ISBN 9780802141187.

Buil, I., Martínez, E., & Matute, J. (2018). Transformational leadership and employee performance: The role of identification, engagement and proactive personality. International Journal of Hospitality Management. Carlyle, Thomas. (1840). On Heroes, Hero Worship, and The Heroic In History. London: Chapman and Hall Ltd.

Carlyle, T. (1849). On heroes, hero-worship, and the heroic in history. Boston: Houghton-Mifflin.

Chemers, Martin M. An integrative theory of leadership. Mahwah, NJ: Lawrence Erlbaum Associates, 1997.

Clark, J.M. (1916). The changing basis of economic responsibility. Journal of Political Economy, 24, 209-119.

Clawson, J. G. (2003). Level three leadership: getting below the surface (2nd ed.). Upper Saddle River, NJ: Prentice Hall.

Collins, Jim. (2001). Good to great: why some companies make the leap and others don't. New York: Harper Business.

Conger, J.A. (1989). The charismatic leader: behind the mystique of exceptional leadership. Jossey-Bass, San Francisco, CA.

Cooper, Paul, Colin J. Smith, and Graham Upton. Emotional and behavioral difficulties: theory to practice. New York: Routledge, 1994.

Day, D.V. and Antonakis, J. (Eds.). (2011). The nature of leadership, 2nd Edition. Thousand Oaks, CA: Sage Publications.

Eagly, A. H.; Johannesen-Schmidt, M. C.; Van Engen, M. L. (2003). "Transformational, transactional, and laissez-faire leadership styles: a meta-analysis comparing women and men" (PDF). Psychological Bulletin. 129 (4): 569–91. doi:10.1037/0033-2909.129.4.569. PMID 12848221.

Encyclopedia of Management (2009). Leadership Theories and Studies. In Encyclopedia of Management. http://www.enotes.com/management-encyclopedia/leadership-theories-studies.

Fiedler, F. E. (1967). A theory of leadership effectiveness. New York: McGraw-Hill.

Fiedler, F. E. (1971). Leadership. Morristown, NJ: General Learning.

Fisk, P. (2002). The making of a digital leader. Business Strategy Review, 13 (1), 43-50.

Fleishman, E.A. (1953). Personnel are people. Personnel Psychology. 6(2), 205–222.

French, J. R. P. Jr. and Raven, B. (1962). The bases of social power. In D. Cartwright (Ed), Group Dynamics: Research and Theory (pp. 259-269). New York: Harper and Row.

Galton, F. (1869). Hereditary genius. New York: Appleton.

George, B., McLean, A.N., & Craig, N. (2008). Finding your true north: a personal guide. San Francisco: Jossey-Bass.

Gerstner, C. R., & Day, D. V. (1997). Meta-analytic review of leader–member exchange theory: Correlates and construct issues. Journal of Applied Psychology, 82, 827–844.

Goleman, D., Boyatzis, R., and McKee, A. (2002). The emotional reality of teams. Journal of Organizational Excellence, 21(2), 55-65.

Graen, G. B., & Uhl-Bien, M. (1995). Relationship-based approach to leadership: development of leader- member exchange (LMX) theory of leadership over 25 years: Applying a multi-level multi-domain perspective. The Leadership Quarterly, 6, 219–247.

Greenleaf, R. K. (1970). The servant as leader. Indianapolis: The Robert K. Greenleaf Center.

Greenleaf, R. K. (1977). Servant leadership: a journey into the nature of legitimate power and greatness. Mahwah, NJ: Paulist Press.

Greenleaf, R. K. (2003). The servant-leader within: a transformative path. New York: Paulist Press.

Gupta, Varun (July–September 2004). "Impact of socialization on transformational leadership: role of leader member exchange" (PDF). South Asian Journal of Management.

Heifetz, R. (1994). Leadership without easy answers, Cambridge, Mass.: Harvard University Press.

Heifetz, R., Kania, J., and Kramer, M. (2004). Leading boldly. Stanford Social Innovation Review, Winter.

Hersey, P. and Blanchard, K. (1969). The life cycle theory of leadership. Training and Development Journal, 23 (5), 26-34.

Hersey, P., Blanchard, K. (1977). Management of Organizational Behavior: Utilizing Human Resources. 3rd ed. New Jersey: Prentice Hall.

Hersey, P. (1985). The situational leader. New York, NY: Warner Books.

House, R.J. (1971). A path-goal theory of leader effectiveness. Administrative Science Quarterly, 16, 321 - 339.

Hughes, R. L., Ginnett, R. D., & Curphy, G. J. (2006). Leadership: Enhancing the lessons of experience (5th ed.). Boston, MA: McGraw Hill.

Ilies, R., Nahrgang, J. D., & Morgeson, F. P. (2007). Leader-member exchange and citizenship behaviors: A meta-analysis. Journal of Applied Psychology, 92, 269–277.

Johnson, Craig E. "Ch. 7: Normative leadership theories" (PDF). Meeting the Ethical Challenges of Leadership. SAGE Publications.

Joyce, E.; Judge, Timothy A. (2004). "Personality and transformational and transactional leadership: a meta-analysis". Journal of Applied Psychology. 89 (5): 901–910. CiteSeerX 10.1.1.692.7909. doi:10.1037/0021-9010.89.5.901. PMID 15506869.

Judge, T. A.; Piccolo, R. F. (2004). "Transformational and transactional leadership: a meta-analytic test of their relative validity" (PDF). The Journal of Applied Psychology. 89 (5): 755–68. doi:10.1037/0021-9010.89.5.755. PMID 15506858.

Kahai, S., Jestire, R., & Rui, H. (2013). "Effects of transformational and transactional leadership on cognitive effort and outcomes during collaborative learning within a virtual world". British Journal of Educational Technology. 44 (6): 969–985. doi:10.1111/bjet.12105.

Kane, Thomas D.; Tremble, Trueman R. (2000). "Transformational leadership effects at different levels of the Army". Military Psychology. 12 (2): 137–160. doi:10.1207/s15327876mp1202_4.

Katz, D., Maccoby, N., Morse, N.C. (1950). Productivity, Supervision and Morale in an Office Situation. Ann Arbor: University of Michigan, Institute of Social Research.

Katz, D., Maccoby, N., Gurin, G., & Floor, L. G. (1951). Productivity, supervision and morale among railroad workers. Ann Arbor, MI: Institute for Social Research, University of Michigan.

Katz, R. L. (1955). Skills of an effective administrator. Harvard Business review, 33 (1), 33-42.

Kelly, Joe, and Louise Kelly. An existential-systems approach to managing organizations. Westport, CT: Quorum Books, 1998.

Kelman, HC. 1958. Compliance, identification, and internalization: three processes of attitude change. Journal of Conflict Resolution. 2(1):51-60.

Kirkpatrick, S. & Locke, E. (1991). Leadership: do traits matter? Academy of Management Executive, May, 48-60.

Koh, William L.; Steers, Richard M.; Terborg, James R. (1995-07-01). "The effects of transformational leadership on teacher attitudes and student performance in Singapore". Journal of Organizational Behavior. 16(4): 319–333. doi:10.1002/job.4030160404.

Kotter, J. P.(1990). Force for change: How leadership differs from management. New York: The Free Press.

Likert, R. (1967). New patterns of management. New York: McGraw-Hill.

Ling, Y; Simseck, Z; Lubatkin, M.H.; Veiga, J.F. (2008). "The impact of transformational CEOs on the performance of small- to medium-sized firms: Does organizational context matter?". Journal of Applied Psychology. 93 (4): 923–34. doi:10.1037/0021-9010.93.4.923. PMID 18642995.

Matthews, Gerald, Ian J. Deary, and Martha C. Whiteman. Personality traits. 2nd ed. Cambridge, England: Cambridge University Press, 2003. Questia. Web. 7 Apr. 2011.

McCaffery, P. (2004). The higher education manager's handbook: effective leadership and management in universities and colleges. London: Routledge Farmer.

McGregor, D. (1960). The human side of enterprise. New York: McGraw-Hill Book Company, Inc.

Miner, John B. Organizational behavior: foundations, theories, and analyses. Oxford: Oxford University Press, 2002.

Mintzberg, H. (1973). The nature of managerial work. New York: Harper and Row.

Mumford, M.D., Zaccaro, S.J., Connelly, M.S., Marks, M.A. (2000). Leadership skills: conclusions and future directions. Leadership Quarterly, 11 (1), 155-70.

Northouse, P. G. (2016). Leadership: theory and practice (7th ed.). Thousand Oaks, CA: Sage Publications.

Owen, Hilarie. In Search of Leaders. New York: John Wiley & Sons, 2000. Questia. Web. 15 Jan. 2011. Sogunro, Olusegun Agboola. "Leadership effectiveness and personality characteristics of group members." Journal of Leadership Studies 5.3 (1998): 26.

Phipps, Simone T.A. (2011). "The influence of personality factors on transformational leadership: exploring the moderating role of political skill" (PDF). International Journal of Leadership Studies.

Riggio, Ronald E. (2009-03-24). "Are you a transformational leader?". Psychology Today.

Robbins, S. P., & Coulter, M. (2002). Management (7th ed.). Upper Saddle River, NJ: Prentice Hall.

Rost, J. C. (1993). Leadership for the twenty-first century. London: Praeger.

Sashkin, M. (1988). The visionary leader. In J. A. Conger and R. N. Kanungo (Eds.). Charismatic leadership: the elusive factor in organizational effectiveness (pp. 122-160). San Francisco: Jossey Bass.

Scouller, J. (2011). The three levels of leadership: how to develop your leadership presence, knowhow, and skill. Cirencester: Management Books. 2000.

Sendjaya, S. (2015) 'Personal and organizational excellence through servant leadership: learning to serve, serving to lead, leading to transform,' Springer.

Sills, D. L. (Ed) (1991). International encyclopedia of the social sciences. New York: Free Press. Smirl, Paul. "Becoming a Transformational Leader". Wisconsin School of Business. Retrieved November 22,2018.

Spears, L.C. (1998) Insights on leadership: service, stewardship, spirit, and servant-leadership. New Your: Wiley.

Spears, L.C. (2010) 'Character and servant leadership: 10 characteristics of effective, caring leaders,' The Journal of Virtues and Leadership, Vol. 1, Issue 1.

Stogdill, R. M. (1974). Handbook of leadership: a survey of theory and research. New York, NY: Free Press.

Stogdill, R. M. (1974). "Personal factors associated with leadership: a survey of the literature." Journal of Psychology 25 (1948): 335-71.

Tannenbaoum, R. and Schmidt, W. (1958). How to choose a leadership pattern. Havard Business Review 36(2), 95-101.

Tafvelin, Susanne (2013) The transformational leadership process antecedents, mechanisms, and outcomes in the social services. PhD Thesis. Umeå University, Faculty of Social Sciences, Department of Psychology.

Taylor, F. W. (1911). The principles of scientific management. New York, NY: Harper & Brothers Publishers.

Tyssen, Ana K.; Wald, Andreas; Heidenreich, Sven (2014). "Leadership in the context of temporary organizations: a study on the effects of transactional and transformational leadership on followers' commitment in projects". Journal of Leadership & Organizational Studies. 21 (4): 376–393. doi:10.1177/1548051813502086.

Vanderpyl, T. (2012) 'Servant leadership: a case study of a canadian healthcare innovator,' Journal of Healthcare Leadership, No 4, 2012.

Vroom, Victor H. & Yetton, Phillip W. (1973). Leadership and Decision-Making. Pittsburgh: University of Pittsburgh Press.

Wang, Gang; Oh, In-Sue; Courtright, Stephen H.; Colbert, Amy E. (2011). "Transformational leadership and performance across criteria and levels: a meta-analytic review of 25 years of research". Group & Organization Management. 36(2): 223–270.

Williams, Michael. Leadership for leaders. London: Thorogood, 2005.

Wyld, David (2013). "Transformation leadership: when is it redundant?". Academy of Management Perspectives. 27 (2). doi:10.5465/amp.2013.0064.

Zaccaro, S. J., Kemp, C., & Bader, P. (2004). Leader traits and attributes. In J. Antonakis, A. T. Cianciolo, & R. J. Sternberg (Eds.). The nature of leadership (pp. 101-124). Thousand Oaks, CA: Sage.

Zineldin, M. (2017). "Transformational leadership behavior, emotions, and outcomes: Health psychology perspective in the workplace". Journal of Workplace Behavioral Health. 32: 14–25. doi:10.1080/15555240.2016.1273782.